"In The Style Of..."

100CLASSICJAZZ
LICKSFORGUITAR

Learn 100 Jazz Guitar Licks In The Style Of 20 Of The World's Greatest Players

JOSEPH**ALEXANDER**

FUNDAMENTAL**CHANGES**

100 Classic Jazz Licks for Guitar

Learn 100 Jazz Guitar Licks In The Style Of 20 Of The World's Greatest Players

Published by www.fundamental-changes.com

ISBN 978-1-78933-020-5

Copyright © 2018 Joseph Alexander

Edited by Tim Pettingale

The moral right of this author has been asserted.

www.fundamental-changes.com

Twitter: **@guitar_joseph**

Over 10,000 fans on Facebook: **FundamentalChangesInGuitar**

Instagram: **FundamentalChanges**

For over 350 Free Guitar Lessons with Videos Check Out

www.fundamental-changes.com

Cover Image Copyright: Shutterstock: Zheltyshev

Contents

Introduction

"In the Style of…?" What does that mean?

To write this book we immersed ourselves in the music of each of the artists covered and spent hours listening to hundreds of tracks. While these one hundred licks are not transcribed directly from the records, they are as stylistically accurate as we can make them.

Each of the five licks for every artist is designed to encapsulate their approach to soloing in a couple of bars. For example, a Wes Montgomery lick in this book should make you say "Ahhh! That's Wes alright!"

Of course, it's impossible to encapsulate the style of a player in just five phrases – the musicians featured here are all talented, complex individuals with rich musical vocabularies; a whole book could be devoted to each one (maybe one day we'll do that)!

Rather, the phrases here are intended as a starting point for your exploration of each guitarist and their music. If you work through all the examples in this book and practise the licks so that you absorb them into your playing, you'll build a comprehensive jazz vocabulary and be well on your way to developing your own style.

You may have bought this book as a shortcut to jazz guitar soloing. We are confident it will help you, especially with the stylistic aspects of each player. Most jazz vocabulary is arpeggio based, but the way that each guitarist makes phrases personal and unique to them is probably the biggest insight this book can give you.

We all expand our vocabulary by copying phrases from other people – it's how language works. So the best practice you can do to take your playing further is to transcribe the solos of your favourite artists. Turn off the cell phone, close Facebook and just sit with your guitar, figuring out the licks you love. Cherry pick the lines that jump out at you and master them, note by note. That way you'll expand your vocabulary in the style you love and, above all, you'll sound like you.

Finally, please download the audio for the book. Reading music off paper is one thing, but you really need to hear each lick to get a feel for how it's played. Jazz is all about feel. While the notation will show you the notes, the audio will give you the all-important phrasing and nuance. Instructions for getting the audio for free are on the next page.

Above all, have fun exploring the music of these incredible jazz guitarists. Apply everything musically and focus on learning what you enjoy hearing.

We had a huge amount of fun putting this book together. We hope it's equally as enjoyable to learn from and provides a unique insight into the music of the guitarists you love.

Good Luck!

Joseph and Pete

How to Use this Book

Our advice is to pick your favourite guitarist and dive right into their licks. Pay attention to the chords each lick is played over, as they have a profound effect on the feeling of the melody. Once you have the basic grasp of a lick, play it over the accompanying backing track to hear how it sounds and focus on the feel. Play it at 1/4 speed if you need to, until you're comfortable, then gradually bring the lick up to speed with the help of a metronome.

Once you're confident, experiment and play the line in different ways. Phrasing is everything, so begin the lick at different points in the bar. How about sliding, or hammer-ons / pull-offs instead of picking? Aim to make each lick your own.

Use each lick as a basis for your own solos. Learn to develop the lick by changing notes, placement, phrasing, extending, contracting… there are hundreds of ways to alter a musical phrase, so trust your ears and have fun; it's impossible to make a mistake! Something can be learned from every lick, even if you just take a small part of it and play it at a different speed, or just capture the general vibe. Treat each lick as a starting point rather than a destination. Explore and see where they take you.

Joseph's book, **Blues Guitar Melodic Phrasing** goes into great depth about all these concepts and more. It teaches you how to develop a personal musical language with soul and great phrasing. You'll learn all about placement and displacement and we recommend it as an ideal companion to this book.

Some of the licks in this book, by more speedy players like Pat Metheny and Mike Stern, are technically demanding, as they are played quickly and include many fast note subdivisions. If these licks are too quick for you right now, don't worry because playing them to tempo is a long-term goal.

For further study of jazz and to get more ideas about how to apply these licks, check out the following books from Fundamental Changes.

- **Beyond Chord Melody with Martin Taylor**

- **Chord Tone Soloing for Jazz Guitar**

- **Fundamental Changes in Jazz Guitar**

- **Minor ii V Mastery**

- **Voice Leading Jazz Guitar**

- **Bebop Jazz Blues Guitar**

- **Jazz Blues Soloing for Guitar**

Get the Audio

The audio files for this book are available to download for free from **www.fundamental-changes.com.** The "Download Audio" link is on the menu at the top right. Click the type of book you've bought (guitar, bass etc). This will take you to a form page where you'll select the title of your book from the drop-down list. Follow the instructions to get the audio.

We recommend that you download the files directly to your computer, not to your tablet, then extract them before adding them to your media library. You can then put them onto your tablet, iPod or burn them to CD. On the download page there is a help PDF and we also provide technical support via the contact form.

For over 350 Free Guitar Lessons with Videos Check out:

www.fundamental-changes.com

Twitter: **@guitar_joseph**

Over 10,000 fans on Facebook: **FundamentalChangesInGuitar**

Instagram: **FundamentalChanges**

Kindle / eReaders

To get the most out of this book, remember that you can **double tap any image to enlarge it**. Turn off column viewing and hold your Kindle in landscape mode.

Get your audio now for free:

www.fundamental-changes.com/download-audio

It makes the book come alive, and you'll learn much more!

If you have a problem, please get in touch before writing a negative review:

response@fundamental-changes.com

The very few negative reviews we receive are normally based around audio/technical issues that we can solve quickly for you!

1. Django Reinhardt

Jean "Django" Reinhardt was born in Belgium on 23rd January 1910 into a family of Manouche Romani (gypsy) descent. Reinhardt spent the majority of his youth in various Romani camps situated around Paris and began his musical career at an early age, initially playing violin, then later the guitar and banjo. It is believed that his father was also musical, playing piano within the family group.

Reinhardt learned guitar quickly and copied many of the musicians he was exposed to, including his uncle who played both guitar and violin. Such was his talent, by the age of 15 he was able to make a living as a performing musician. His first recordings (playing the banjo-guitar) were made in 1928 accompanying three accordionists and a singer called Maurice Chaumel. Reinhardt's reputation as a fluid and inventive guitarist grew rapidly and he soon came to the attention of musicians outside of France, including the British bandleader Jack Hylton who subsequently offered him a job.

Reinhardt's musical plans were tragically cut short when a fire ravaged the caravan where he lived with his wife. His injuries were so severe that doctors suggested amputating one of his legs (he refused the procedure) and he lost the use of two of his fretting fingers which were paralysed. For many, this would have been the end of their playing career, but Reinhardt was determined to overcome his injuries. He taught himself to play again using only his index and middle fingers and thumb. With the aid of a new instrument bought for him by his brother, Joseph (also a guitarist), he also learned to incorporate his paralysed fingers for chord work.

After separating from his wife, he travelled widely throughout France leading a rather austere existence playing small venues for little money. It was only later when he discovered American jazz music and met the violinist Stephane Grappelli that his fortunes changed for the better. Grappelli and Reinhardt began jamming regularly and soon formed The Hot Club, which became one of the most innovative jazz ensembles of the pre-war era in Europe. The arrival of war in 1939 signified the end of The Hot Club group and Reinhardt returned to Paris, with Grappelli remaining in the UK. The Nazi persecution of the gypsies and their general distaste for jazz music presented a dangerous threat to Reinhardt, but he managed to survive the war and continued to compose and play where and when he could.

After the war, Reinhardt reunited with Grappelli and also undertook a tour in the US as a guest soloist with Duke Ellington before returning to France in 1947. The following few years sadly saw Reinhardt become increasingly unreliable as a performer and he frequently missed even his own sold-out concerts if he suddenly chose not to perform. Despite this erratic behaviour, he continued to record and perform into the late 1940s, including a 1949 recording session in Rome and also a brief period alongside Benny Goodman who wanted Reinhardt to work with him in the US.

Reinhardt's last years were mostly spent playing in Paris jazz clubs and living in semi-retirement at Samois-sur-Seine, near Fontainebleau. He began working with an electric guitar and his playing also took on more of a bebop flavour that can be heard in his final recordings. These were made just before he died of a brain haemorrhage in 1951. He was only 43 years old.

Since the mid-1960s there has been a revival of interest in Reinhardt's music – a movement that has continued to the present day with numerous annual festivals and tribute concerts. His devotees included classical guitarist Julian Bream and country guitarist Chet Atkins, who considered him one of the ten greatest guitarists of the twentieth century.

Reinhardt almost exclusively used Selmer acoustic guitars during his career and rarely used an electric guitar. Selmer guitars were typical gypsy jazz instruments with an oval sound hole and usually a medium-to-high string action. Reinhardt played with a heavy tortoiseshell pick.

Reinhardt's soloing style was based around a combination of arpeggios and chromatic approach notes. These were executed with great technical skill and rhythmic drive, despite his finger injuries. His astonishing technical skills on the instrument are all the more remarkable considering his physical limitation.

Recommended Listening

Django Reinhardt and the Hot Club Quintet

The Great Artistry of Django Reinhardt

At Club St Germain

The first Django Reinhardt lick is a typical gypsy jazz chord move, which involves shifting a chord voicing up or down chromatically to arrive at the next required chord.

Example 1a begins with a quick slide from the 4th to 3rd position in bar one, then the Am6 chord shape is moved up the neck one fret at a time to arrive at the 9th position on the up-beat of beat 4 in the second bar. The chord form has become Dm6 and matches the change to D minor in the backing music.

With these quick chord movements, make sure you play the voicings accurately and in time. Also make sure that the destination chord is correct for the harmony of the composition! You will find that if you play the top three strings in each chord by barring with your third finger, the chord form is easier to move at speed.

Example 1a

Like most gypsy jazz players, Django used lots of arpeggios in his playing, which is especially useful when soloing over fast-tempo tunes. The next example looks deceptively simple on paper, but illustrates two trademark Django soloing approaches. The line begins with an A minor arpeggio in the 8th position, followed by a descending sequence of fourth intervals.

In bar three, notice the half-step bend on the B string 7th fret that resolves in bar four to the minor 3rd of the D minor chord. Django never used large interval bends in his playing. It may have been impractical to do so because of the heavy gauged strings he used, but short bends have become a trademark of the gypsy jazz sound.

Example 1b

Reinhardt made effective use of melodic motifs, such as in bar one of Example 1c. It is built around just two notes of an A minor arpeggio (the b3 and 5th), before the full triad is played in bar two.

In bar three, a triplet breaks up the rhythmic flow before the line returns to 1/8th and 1/4 notes. The C# note on beat 3, bar three is an approach note that leads to the root of the D minor chord. The lick concludes with the major 3rd of the E7 chord in bar five, highlighting the chord change.

Listen to the audio example and notice how this line swings. The combination of 1/8th and 1/4 notes gives the motif a forward motion. Practise the line and aim to get that *push* and *pull* swing feeling into your phrasing.

Example 1c

Django frequently used fast chromatic passages in his solos – a device many jazz guitarists would later emulate. Often, he would play a chromatic scale in triplets, as in Example 1d. Again, this lick looks fairly simple on paper, but your challenge is to play it cleanly and accurately at the required tempo, and this will take some patience.

Note that although the scale is played in triplets, the line is arranged in a four note per string pattern. Concentrate on getting your fingering correct, then practise the lick slowly, gradually bringing it up to tempo. (Many gypsy jazz guitarists will play chromatic runs on a single string, but this requires great control and lots of practise!)

Example 1d

Example 1e begins with an Am7 arpeggio in the 5th position in bar one, before a hammer-on and pull-off triplet figure arrives on beat 1 of bar two. You can hear Django make effective use of triplets in his recordings, in order to avoid playing predictable 1/8th or 1/4 note passages all the time.

When playing this line, be careful with the position shift which is required for the short melody beginning on beat 3 of bar three and finishing on bar four.

Bars five and six feature a favourite melodic device of gypsy jazz: the use of a diminished arpeggio over a dominant 7th chord. In this lick, a B diminished arpeggio (B D F G#) is played over the E7 chord. Superimposing a Bdim arpeggio over E7 gives the 5th, b7, b9 and 3rd intervals – in effect, an E7b9 chord with no root note.

Once again, play this arpeggio slowly and make sure each note sounds cleanly before increasing the tempo.

Example 1e

2. Charlie Christian

Charles Henry "Charlie" Christian was born in Bonham, Texas in July 1916 and moved with his family to Oklahoma while he was still a child. Both Christian's parents were active musicians and his father taught him and his two older brothers the basics of music. He also encouraged them to work as buskers to earn some extra money for the family. Following his father's early death, Christian inherited his instruments and continued to study music at home. Whilst attending school in Oklahoma City, he initially began playing trumpet (encouraged by one of his music teachers) but later dropped the instrument as he was more interested in playing baseball at the time.

During the 1920s and '30s, Christian's older brother Edward led a band in Oklahoma City and his other brother, Clarence, arranged for the young Christian to have secret guitar lessons from "Bigfoot" Ralph Hamilton where he was taught to play and solo on three well known songs of the era: *Sweet Georgia Brown*, *Tea For Two* and *Rose Room*. Christian became so adept at playing these tunes that when he was eventually invited to play at a late night jam session in Oklahoma City with Edward's band, his playing was greatly praised by the audience.

This successful early performance helped Christian gain regular performance work throughout the Midwest and by the mid-1930s he was attracting considerable attention within the region. By now he was playing an early model Gibson electric guitar. Around this period his guitar playing skills also came to the notice of the record producer John Hammond, who recommended Christian to the legendary swing bandleader Benny Goodman.

In 1939, after some initial reservations about using an electric guitarist in his group, Goodman formed a new sextet featuring Christian on guitar. His fluid playing immediately drew praise from other jazz musicians, who noted his "horn-like" approach to guitar. Later he stated that he deliberately wanted to sound more like a saxophone than a traditional guitarist. By 1940 Christian was regularly topping swing jazz and guitar polls, even though he was still comparatively young. He was also invited to join the Metronome All Stars (an elite group of jazz musicians assembled for studio recordings by Metronome magazine).

Outside of his work with Goodman, Charlie Christian was a significant figure in the early development of bebop jazz, often appearing at the famous Minton's Playhouse club in Harlem (considered by many to be the birthplace of bebop). His highly melodic style influenced many of the most significant bebop performers of the next decade, such as Charlie Parker and Dizzy Gillespie.

Sadly, Christian's hectic touring and performance schedule through the 1930s and '40s eventually took a toll on his health and after he contracted tuberculosis in the late 1930s, he had several stays in various hospitals to try and recover his health. Eventually he was admitted to a care facility in New York in June 1941 and died early the next year aged only 25.

Christian's influence on later-era musicians is significant and many well-known players of the 1950s and '60s cite him as a major influence on their playing, including musicians outside of the jazz world. Most musicologists agree that he paved the way for the electric guitar to become a lead solo instrument in jazz, rather than remaining an instrument for rhythmic accompaniment.

Christian's playing style expertly mixed blues riffs with longer 1/8th note lines (often with chromatic passing tones) all played with impeccable timing and phrase construction. You can hear the elements of early bebop in his swing solos with Goodman.

Charlie Christian played a Gibson ES-150 guitar. It was the first electric guitar to achieve commercial success for the Gibson Company, due in no small part to Christian's use of the instrument. The guitar featured a single-coil neck position pickup that has since become known simply as the "Charlie Christian Pickup". He would have used heavy gauge strings as lighter gauges were not available during his playing career. For amplification he used a Gibson EH150 amp which featured a 10" (or later a 12") speaker and produced about 15 watts.

Recommended Listening

Solo Flight: The Genius of Charlie Christian

Electric

Charlie Christian with the Benny Goodman Sextet and Orchestra

Charlie Christian was a melodic player and frequently used repeating motifs to build his solos. In Example 2a, a simple two note motif begins in bar one, preceded by an approach note, and emphasises the 6th and root of the C major chord. This motif continues in bar two, but is now played over a C#dim chord. Notice the tension the notes create against the new chord.

In bar three, a short C major scale sequence is played over the G7 chord, beginning with a triplet figure on beat 1. The lick concludes with the b7 of the same chord – a strong chord tone.

Despite the relative simplicity of this line, it demonstrates just how effective a well thought-out melody can be. When playing this line, aim to capture Christian's sense of rhythmic authority and emphasis of the chord tones.

Example 2a

Christian often used chromatic passing notes in his solos to drive melodic movement. In bar one of Example 2b, an Ab is played on the fourth 1/8 note beat, which targets the 5th interval of the C major chord. Another passing note is played on the final beat of the bar which leads to the E note at the beginning of bar two.

This is followed by a diminished arpeggio – a common approach of swing players of this era and used by Django Reinhardt as previously noted. Bar three uses an inverted Dm7 arpeggio substituted against the G7 chord, and a combined triplet and 1/8th note phrase concludes the lick.

When playing this line, watch out for the position shift midway through bar two as you move from 8th to 5th position. Also take care with the phrasing in bar two and listen to the audio example to hear how it should sound.

Example 2b

This next line illustrates how swing players heavily influenced the bebop players that would follow. Example 2c begins with a one-bar phrase that has become stock vocabulary for jazz and blues. A passing note targets the E note on beat 2 of bar one, before a quick triplet figure leads to the root of the C major chord. Bar two utilises a descending diminished arpeggio pattern many swing players used. The lick finishes with a simple three note motif highlighting the 4th, 5th and 9th degrees of the G7 chord.

Make sure you have practised and internalised the fingering of the diminished pattern in bar two before taking the lick up to tempo.

Example 2c

The opening double-stops of Example 2d could easily have come from a 1950s Rock'n'Roll recording, but were a regular feature of Christian's playing from over a decade earlier. For maximum authenticity, try to bend the top E string fractionally sharp to make the bend sound bluesy. Use your fourth finger to play the top E string and your third finger to play the B string for the double-stops.

As in previous examples, a diminished arpeggio is played over the C#dim chord in bar two, but here is played beginning on an upbeat to help the line swing more. In the final two bars, a simple three note figure is played over the G7 chord and the last note is the 6th degree of the chord.

Be extra careful not to rush this lick as it relies on being played accurately, with a solid sense of time and swing feel.

Example 2d

The final Charlie Christian lick has a simple rhythmic construction and should not present a great technical challenge to play. But, despite its simplicity, it is rich in harmony.

Bar one targets the root and 6th of the C major chord. This is followed by a three-note motif in bar two, drawn from a C#dim arpeggio. A series of descending 1/4 notes are played over G7 for the final two bars.

These cascading 1/4 notes suggest a G13 arpeggio. In descending order the intervals played are the 13th, 5th, 9th, b7, 5th, 11th and 3rd of the G7 chord. Like many swing era players, Christian was beginning to explore the chord substitutions that would become an essential part of the bebop jazz vocabulary in the late 1940s.

Example 2e

3. Herb Ellis

Mitchell Herbert "Herb" Ellis was born in Farmersville, Texas on August 4, 1921 and raised in a Dallas suburb. Ellis was first exposed to the electric guitar listening to a performance by guitarist George Barnes on a radio program and it is believed that this inspired him to take up the guitar. He quickly became proficient on the instrument and entered North Texas State University to major in music. As the university did not have a guitar program at the time, he had to study string bass and subsequently, due to lack of money, he was forced to drop out of college. Ellis then elected to tour for six months with a band from the University of Kansas. Around this time he also became aware of the guitar playing of Charlie Christian, who became one of his biggest musical influences.

In 1943, Ellis joined the Casa Loma Orchestra and it was with this band that he received his first recognition in the jazz world. Following this he joined the Jimmy Dorsey group where he recorded some of his first guitar solos to appear on an album. Ellis remained with Dorsey through 1947, travelling and recording extensively and playing in dance halls and movie theatres.

Ellis' career took a major upswing when, during a six-week break in the Dorsey band's touring schedule, he got together with pianist Lou Carter and bassist John Frigo to form the group Soft Winds, gaining a six month residency at the Peter Stuyvesant Hotel in Buffalo. The group stayed together until 1952 and were modelled on the Nat King Cole Trio. Together with Frigo and Lou Carter, Ellis also wrote the classic jazz standard *Detour Ahead*.

Ellis then moved on to join the celebrated jazz pianist Oscar Peterson (replacing guitarist Barney Kessel) in 1953, forming one of the most celebrated jazz trios of all time, alongside bassist Ray Brown. Incidentally, Ellis was the only white member of the trio – a fact that was quite controversial at the time.

The Peterson trio (often with the addition of a drummer) became the regular house band for Norman Granz's Verve Records, supporting many popular jazz musicians of the era. Ellis mostly played as part of the rhythm section for these Verve recordings and did not always have a featured solo.

The Peterson trio were also one of the mainstays of the "Jazz at the Philharmonic" concerts organised by Granz and toured constantly in both the United States and Europe. Ellis finally left the trio in November 1958, to be replaced by drummer Ed Thigpen rather than another guitarist. After the Peterson gig ended, Ellis became more involved with studio sessions and was often featured in the house band for TV programmes such as the Steve Allen Show.

Between 1957 and 1960, Ellis toured and performed extensively with the legendary jazz singer Ella Fitzgerald and later formed the Great Guitars trio with fellow guitarists Barney Kessel, Charlie Byrd and Tal Farlow. In the 1970s he began increasing the number of his live performances and also formed a fruitful musical partnership with fellow jazz guitarist Joe Pass. In 1982, Ellis formed the group Triple Threat with Monty Alexander and Ray Brown and this group continued working together well into the 1990s.

In 1994, Ellis joined the Arkansas Jazz Hall of Fame and on November 15, 1997, he received an Honorary Doctorate in Music from the University of North Texas.

Ellis sadly passed way from Alzheimer's disease at his Los Angeles home on the morning of March 28, 2010, at the age of 88.

Although initially influenced by the guitar playing of Charlie Christian, Herb Ellis developed into a fluid swing/bop soloist in his own right. His grasp of harmony and uncanny ability to swing even at the fast tempos of the Oscar Peterson trio, drew much praise over the years and he remains one of the major figures of jazz guitar in the 20th century.

Herb Ellis favoured archtop jazz guitars such as the Gibson ES-175 and the ES-165 and also had a signature Aria Pro II Herb Ellis model made for him. His choice of amplifier was generally a small clean-toned combo (often solid-state, such as the Polytone Mini-Brute) and was also known to have played Ampeg amps earlier in his career. Ellis rarely, if ever, used effects on his guitar sound, preferring to play straight into his amplifier

Recommended Listening

Ellis in Wonderland

Man with the Guitar

Straight Tracks

Herbs Ellis was equally at home with swing and bebop styles and had impeccable jazz time feel. Example 3a illustrates how Herb could take a melodic pattern and adapt it to last several bars to great effect.

On beat 1 of bar one, a pattern begins which highlights two chord tones of the Fm7 chord, using an approach note a semitone below. The pattern is then transposed to fit the Bbm7 chord in bar two. Play both these bars in 5th position before shifting up to 6th position for bar three.

The pattern from bars one and two continues briefly in bar three, and targets the b9 interval against the Eb7 chord. There is a diminished flavour to the remainder of bar three before the line finishes with a short swing style melody over the Abmaj7 and Dbmaj7 chords.

The constant 1/8th note pattern means there is nothing too technical about this lick. The main challenge is to keep the swing feel when playing at full tempo. Watch out for the position shift required between bars two and three.

Example 3a

Example 3b demonstrates Ellis' use of repeating rhythmic motifs. Beginning on beat 4 of bar one, a combination of 1/8th note triplets and 1/4 notes is played over the first three chords. Notice that motif is not always played on the same beat in each subsequent bar. Rhythm and note placement adds variety to phrasing and builds interest for the listener.

From beat 4 in bar three, a series of tied 1/8th and 1/4 notes builds the rhythmic momentum. A chord tone is targeted on the downbeat of each new bar. Make sure to play this lick with a strong swing feel and don't rush it.

Example 3b

Ellis often used a combination of on and off-beat 1/8th notes to create interest in an otherwise straightforward scale sequence, as Example 3c demonstrates. The offbeat notes really make the line swing. Refer to the audio example to ensure you place the notes on the correct beat during the first three bars.

In bar three, the line continues with a combination of 1/8th and 1/4 notes, but includes some tied notes (such as on beat 1 of bar five). The lick resolves to the major 3rd of the Cmaj7 chord in bar seven, before finishing with an interval targeting the major 7th and 5th.

Example 3c

This next lick uses the common bebop approach note technique. Starting with the Fm7 in bar one, the chord tones are approached with notes a scale step above and a semitone below, thus "enclosing" the chord tone. The rhythm of the line is varied as it progresses to prevent it sounding too much like an exercise.

A change of melodic direction occurs in bar six, with a straightforward scale run in C major. The embellishments return again in bars seven and eight with a Charlie Parker style line. In bar seven, the approach notes target the 5th, root and major 3rd of the C major chord. Practise this lick slowly to begin with, focusing on the rhythmic placement of the notes.

Example 3d

The final Ellis style lick demonstrates Herb's tendency to combine chords and single note lines in his solos – a technique he probably developed when playing in trios where his guitar was the only harmonic instrument. Punctuating solos with chordal phrases or stabs can provide a great contrast to long scale or arpeggio runs.

In bars one and two, the Fm7 and Bbm7 chords are played with drop 2 voicings, before an Ab major scale run is introduced in bar three over the Eb7 chord.

A chord tone is played on the first beat of bars four and five to strongly outline the chords, followed by a quick pull-off triplet on beat 3 of bar six. The line ends with drop 2 voicings over the Cmaj7 chord – the second of which is Em7, a common harmonic substitution for Cmaj7.

Example 3e

4. Tal Farlow

Talmage Holt "Tal" Farlow was born in Greensboro in June 1921. He was largely self-taught on guitar, which he only began playing around the age of 22. Farlow was brought up in a musical household – his father played several fretted instruments and his mother and sister both played the piano. He reputedly learned chord melodies by playing a mandolin tuned like a ukulele. Farlow later stated that playing the ukulele provided the initial motivation for using the higher four strings on his guitar for melodies and chords, while the two lowest strings were employed for basslines played with the thumb.

Despite his musical talent, Farlow's only professional training was as a sign painter and he continued this work throughout his life in parallel with his guitar playing. While he was a sign-painting apprentice he requested night shifts at a local shop so that he could listen to popular jazz big bands on the radio. Farlow was initially influenced by early jazz artists such as Bix Beiderbecke, Eddie Lang and Louis Armstrong, but Charlie Christian became his primary influence when he heard him playing electric guitar with Benny Goodman. Farlow later said that he made his own electric guitar because he couldn't afford to buy one at the time.

During WWII, Farlow was stationed in Greensboro and began working with a number of local jazz musicians. Shortly after, while playing with the vibraphonist Dardanelle, he began a residency at the Copacabana Lounge in New York. While in New York, Farlow took the opportunity to hear many of his favourite jazz musicians play on 52 Street – amongst them Charlie Parker, Dizzy Gillespie and pianist Bud Powell. Farlow eventually took an apartment on West 93rd Street in New York, an area popular with other rising stars of the NY jazz scene.

Farlow first came to significant public attention in 1949 when he joined a trio with vibes player Red Norvo and bassist Charles Mingus (he replaced Mundell Lowe on guitar). The Red Norvo Trio became one of the most popular jazz attractions of the 1950s and Farlow's playing was quickly noted and praised by other jazz musicians. Norvo had a habit of playing fast tempos and Farlow's guitar technique soon rose to the challenge. He was awarded the *Down Beat* New Star Award in 1954 and the Critics Poll in 1956.

Farlow left the Norvo trio in 1953 to join the Gramercy Five led by Artie Shaw, and two years later he formed his own trio with bassist Vinnie Burke and vibraphonist Eddie Costa, playing regularly in New York City at the Composers Club in Manhattan. After getting married in 1958, Farlow partially retired from the music scene and settled in Sea Bright, New Jersey. Although he continued to play with a variety of musicians in local clubs, for the most part he returned to his a career as a sign painter. Farlow only made one album as a leader between 1960 and 1975, although in 1962 the Gibson Guitar Corporation (with Farlow's participation) produced the Tal Farlow model.

During the 1970s, Farlow participated in some recordings and undertook a little touring, but was largely out of the limelight until the 1980s when he made six recordings for the Concord label and began playing much further afield than he had in the previous decade and a half. He toured in both Europe and Japan and a documentary film about him was released in 1981.

Farlow continued to perform and record until the mid-1990s, although he curtailed his international touring to concentrate on concerts and teaching in the US. He also deputised for Barney Kessel, Charlie Bryd or Herb Ellis in the Great Guitars group.

Farlow passed away from cancer at Memorial Sloan-Kettering Cancer Centre in New York City on July 25, 1998, at the age of 77.

Farlow was nicknamed "the Octopus" because of his large hands and fast technique over the fretboard. In contrast to other players of his generation, he frequently placed single notes together in clusters, and was able to form chords most other players couldn't achieve due to his large hand size. He developed a great facility with artificial harmonics and often used the guitar's body as a form of percussion.

Farlow used a variety of guitars including his signature Gibson Tal Farlow model, a Gibson ES-250 and an ES-350. For amplifiers he used Fender combos like the Deluxe Reverb and Twin, as well as Gibson amps and a Walter Woods amp.

Recommended Listening

The Artistry of Tal Farlow

Autumn in New York

The Return of Tal Farlow

Tal Farlow was a master of chord melody playing and voice-leading. Example 4a demonstrates his approach to playing a II V I progression in F major. The chord sequence begins with a Gm9 voicing on beat 1 of bar one, which is followed by a series of off-beat bass notes and chords. Note the use of the common tone (a D note on the B string, 3rd fret) that sits on top of the Am11, Ab7b5 and Gm7 chords. The original Gm9 voicing is played again in bar two, beat 3 and a C13b9 chord sets up the final resolution to F6/9.

Listen to the audio example closely, because this passage is played rubato (not to a strict tempo). Strive to play the chords as cleanly as possible and let each note ring for its full rhythmic value. The lick can be played either with a pick or fingerstyle.

Example 4a

Example 4b demonstrates the type of thing Farlow might typically play unaccompanied as an introduction. In bar one, a pedal tone is used (the open A string) under a series of ascending diatonic triads (A minor, B minor, C major).

In bar two a D13b9 chord is sustained for three beats until a series of descending 13th chords are introduced on beat 4 of the same bar. Farlow often used his left hand thumb to play bass notes (due to the size of his hands). Experiment to see whether this technique works for you.

This example is also played rubato, so let each note of the chords ring as much as possible. You can use this line as an outro as well as an intro, especially when playing solo.

Example 4b

Aside from his chord-melody skills, Farlow was an inventive and melodic single line soloist. Example 4c is a seven-bar line played over the chord changes to a well-known jazz standard. Like most master improvisers, Farlow made great use of motifs. In bar one a short motif outlines the chord tones of Em7b5 before resolving to the 3rd and b9 of the A7 chord in bar two.

The motif from bar one is modified slightly in bar three to fit the Cm7 chord, before a scale run is played over the F7 chord in bar four. In bar five the line continues after a two beat rest. Another short scale passage is played over the bar-line between bars five and six, before the line ends with the 3rd and 7th of the Ebmaj7 chord.

The tempo is quite fast here, so learn this line slowly and gradually work up to full speed.

Example 4c

Great bop style soloing isn't all about playing long streams of 1/8th notes. Bars one and two of Example 4d show how Farlow carefully arranged rhythms to make a simple scale descent sound musical. Beginning on the up-beat of beat 1, the line uses alternating off-beats and 1/4 notes throughout the first two bars before it moves to more conventional note placement in bar three. A triplet figure is played in bar three to add rhythmic variety. Farlow used this kind of syncopation often in his playing, especially at faster tempos.

Most great jazz soloists play strong chord tones on downbeats and this is especially noticeable in bars three, six, seven and eight in this lick. Since this is a long line, learn it in small sections, then bring them together. Ensure you can play the whole line fluidly before bringing it up to tempo. Refer to the audio example to nail the timing.

Example 4d

When playing fast lines, Farlow would use occasionally legato phrasing instead of picking every note. This line begins with a descending pull-off from the 12th to 9th fret on the top E string. Try playing this from your little finger to your first, and aim to sound each note with equal volume.

Bar two uses a simple sounding but effective sequence that targets the #5 and 3rd of the A7 chord before a hammer-on and pull-off triplet figure on beat 1 of the final bar. The lick finishes with a brief interval phrase that highlights the b7 and 6th of the Cm7 chord.

Using a combination of legato and picked phrases really helps give a solo dynamic and tonal variety. As with the other licks in this chapter, take your time and learn the line slowly before attempting it at the full tempo.

Example 4e

5. Johnny Smith

John Henry Smith II was born on June 25, 1922 in Birmingham, Alabama. His family moved several times during the Great Depression period and eventually settled in Portland, Maine. It has been recorded that Smith actually taught himself to play guitar whilst working in various local pawnshops. He was allowed to practice in return for keeping the instruments in tune and in good order. He also played the violin. Smith progressed rapidly as a musician and was teaching students by his early teens. He received his first guitar as a gift from one of his pupils.

Smith's first performances were playing country music and he joined Uncle Lem and the Mountain Boys, a local hillbilly group that played regularly around Maine, performing at local dances and fairs. He dropped out of high school to concentrate on his work with the group, especially as he was able to earn around four dollars a night! But Smith's musical tastes gradually moved away from country music and he became increasingly interested in the jazz groups he was hearing on local radio. Aged 18 he left The Mountain Boys to join a trio called The Airport Boys.

Aside from his music, Smith had learned to fly and had hoped to become a military pilot when he enlisted in the United States Army Air Corps. This wasn't to be due to imperfect vision in his left eye, so he was given the choice of joining a military band or being sent to train as a mechanic. Smith opted to join the military band and had to quickly learn the cornet via an instructional book. He had passed the entrance examination for the band within two weeks.

Returning to the guitar as his main instrument after WWII, now with good sight-reading skills, Smith began his professional career in earnest when he accepted an invitation to join the music staff at NBC in New York. As a studio guitarist and arranger for NBC from 1946 to 1951, and on a freelance basis thereafter until 1958, he played in a variety of settings from solo to a full orchestra. Smith also had his own trio, The Playboys, with Mort Lindsey and Arlo Hults. The guitarist also found himself participating in concert recitals of atonal music, such as Schoenberg's Serenade for Septet in 1949 and Berg's opera Wozzeck in 1951 with Dimitri Mitropoulos.

Smith's most critically acclaimed recording is *Moonlight in Vermont* from 1952 (winning one of *Down Beat* magazine's top jazz records for that year), which also featured saxophonist Stan Getz. His best known composition is *Walk Don't Run*, written originally for a 1954 recording session as counter melody to the chord changes of *Softly as in a Morning Sunrise*. This piece became a hit for the group The Ventures who first heard the composition when it was covered by guitarist Chet Atkins. The Ventures' version occupied the No2 slot on the Billboard Top 100 for a week in September 1960.

Earlier in 1957, Smith's wife had tragically died in childbirth, along with his second child. He sent his surviving daughter to Colorado Springs to be cared for temporarily by his mother, then the following year he left his performing career in New York City to join his daughter. Thereafter Smith left the limelight of the NYC music scene to run a musical instrument store, teach music, and raise his daughter. He did, however, continue to record albums for the Royal Roost and Verve labels into the 1960s.

Smith continued to record a little and perform live in Colorado nightclubs, but declined almost all invitations to tour and was largely ignored by the jazz press as a result. In the late 1960s, he recorded three albums for Verve and launched his ground-breaking and popular Guitar Seminars across the US.

One exception he made to his self-imposed exile was for Bing Crosby, who he accompanied on a tour of the US and UK in 1976/77 that ended shortly before Crosby's death. In 1998, Johnny Smith was awarded the prestigious James Smithson Bicentennial Medal in recognition of his influence as a guitarist upon popular culture. Smith died of complications from a fall at his home in Colorado Springs, Colorado, at the age of 90.

Smith was one of the most versatile guitarists of the 1950s. His playing was characterised by close-position piano-like chord voicings and rapidly ascending melodic lines. He possessed an astonishing picking technique and was one of the most technically advanced players of his generation, often playing fast scale and arpeggio lines that spanned three octaves. His solo chord-melody arrangements stand out as some of the best composed for plectrum guitar.

Guild, Gibson, and Heritage all made guitars designed and endorsed by Johnny Smith. In comparison to other jazz guitarists with signature models, each guitar was designed wholly or in part by Smith himself. Smith claims to have learned about guitar design by observing expert luthier John D'Angelico, who was his friend and supplier when he lived in New York. Smith was also involved in amplifier designs and collaborated with Ampeg on the Fountain of Sound amp in the 1950s, and later in the 1960s with Gibson on their GA-75L amplifier.

Recommended Listening

Moonlight In Vermont (with Stan Getz)

The Guitar World of Johnny Smith

Walk, Don't Run

Johnny Smith possessed a flawless pick technique and regularly used long arpeggio and scale runs in his soloing, as demonstrated in bars one and two of Example 5a. In bar one, the F Major scale is played from the 7th degree and ascends to the root. The scale changes to Ab Major in bar two (or the Eb Mixolydian mode) to accommodate the key change. Notice that in both bars, the run begins on a strong chord tone.

In bars three and four, the scale choice changes to G Harmonic Minor for the Am7b5 and D7 chords. This is a popular choice among jazz musicians and suggests a D7b9 sound over the V chord. A Gm7 arpeggio completes the lick. When playing this line, focus on the phrasing and try not to rush the scale runs.

Example 5a

Example 5b is a six-bar line that begins with a trademark Smith arpeggio run that outlines the Fmaj7 chord, then combines several of his favourite soloing approaches.

In bar two, the b7 of the Eb7 chord is targeted on beat 1 to emphasis the key change. On beats 2 and 3, the #11 is highlighted (an A note on the B string, 10th fret). Smith often favoured playing the #11 over dominant chords.

In bars three and four, the G Harmonic Minor scale is used with the addition of chromatic passing notes (the Ab note on beat 4, bar three, which occurs again on the final 1/8th note of bar four).

The lick concludes with a series of off-beat third intervals played as double-stops.

Example 5b

Smith used double-stops to provide a contrast to his single note passages. Example 5c uses them to outline the underlying harmony. Of particular interest here is the rhythmic placement of the double-stops, which are mostly played on off-beats. When adopting an idea like this into your playing, ensure that chord tones are present within the intervals so that you don't lose sight of the harmony.

Bar one targets the 3rd and 5th of Fmaj7 on beat 1, then the root and 3rd on the up-beat of beat 2. In bar two, a common tone of Db is held on the G string (6th fret) while the D string is used to descend down the Ab Major scale. After targeting the b3rd and root of the Am7b5 chord on beat 1 of bar three, the lick finishes with diatonic intervals outlining a D7b9 chord. The notes in the last bar are taken from the G Harmonic Minor scale.

Example 5c

Example 5d demonstrates Johnny Smith's unique approach to chord melody playing. As heard in his famous recording of *Moonlight in Vermont*, Smith favoured close-position voicings that required some unusually large left-hand stretches. Take careful note of the tab fingerings with these chords (especially in bars one and three) and learn each chord in isolation before putting them all together. Bar one requires some significant position shifts from the 10th fret region to the 5th position, so work on this slowly at first.

This chordal passage would work as either an intro or ending in the key of C Major. Don't be put off by the time signature changes. Unaccompanied chord solos often sound like they are being played in different times, but the overall aim is to sound as though it is being played freely.

Example 5d

The final Johnny Smith lick uses the double-stop approach of previous examples and begins with a series of 3rds that move from the 4th to 9th position. Smith often played passages like this in his unaccompanied chord-melody solos. Try playing this lick both picked and fingerstyle. A pick and fingers hybrid approach can also work well.

The final up-beat of bar one is simply a chromatic interval move to arrive at the D7 chord on beat 1 of bar two. The whole passage is a II V I progression in G Major. Bar two uses a D13b9 voicing (constructed from the D half-whole diminished scale) to set up the final cadence to the G6/9 chord in the last bar.

This line demonstrates how Smith would use chord substitutions and chordal embellishment to decorate a familiar sequence.

Example 5e

6. Wes Montgomery

John Leslie "Wes" Montgomery was born in March 1923 in Indianapolis, USA. Montgomery came from a musical family and his two brothers, Monk and Buddy, both became noted jazz musicians in their own right. The nickname Wes was apparently a childhood abbreviation of his middle name, Leslie. Montgomery began learning guitar at the relatively late age of 19 by listening to and learning from the recordings of the guitarist Charlie Christian. He had, however, previously played a four-string tenor guitar from the age of 12. He was self-taught and famously played with his thumb rather than using a pick.

Montgomery was celebrated early in his career for his ability to play Christian's solos note for note and was reputedly hired by the vibraphonist and bandleader Lionel Hampton for this ability. Although he was not a proficient sight-reader, Montgomery could quickly absorb complex melodies and jazz harmonies by ear alone. He toured with Lionel Hampton's orchestra from July 1948 to January 1950, but was unhappy with the lengthy touring and working away from his family, so soon returned home to Indianapolis.

By now with a family of eight to support, Montgomery worked in a local factory each day from 7:00am to 3:00pm, then performed in local clubs until 2:00am. The saxophonist Cannonball Adderley heard Montgomery in an Indianapolis club and was sufficiently impressed with his playing to contact record producer Orrin Keepnews, who signed Montgomery to a recording contract with Riverside Records in 1959.

Montgomery was with Riverside until 1963, and the recordings made during this period are widely considered by jazz historians to be amongst Montgomery's best work. Two particular recording sessions in January 1960 contributed to the album *The Incredible Jazz Guitar of Wes Montgomery*, which was recorded as a quartet. The album featured two of his best-known compositions, *Four on Six* and *West Coast Blues*. Nearly all of Montgomery's work on Riverside features him in a small group setting, playing a mixture of up-tempo standards/originals and quiet expressive ballads.

In 1964 Montgomery moved to Verve Records for two years. His stay at Verve yielded a number of albums where he was featured with an orchestra, including *Movin' Wes*, *Bumpin* and *California Dreaming*. While some critics bemoaned Montgomery's apparent move from straight-ahead jazz to a more commercial pop platform, Montgomery never abandoned jazz entirely during his Verve years, and evidence can be heard on recordings such as the 1965 live album *Smokin' at the Half Note* with the Wynton Kelly Trio. He also recorded with the jazz organist Jimmy Smith on several albums including *Jimmy & Wes: The Dynamic Duo* and *Further Adventures of Jimmy and Wes*.

Montgomery was also invited to join legendary saxophonist John Coltrane's group, but elected instead to continue his solo work. By 1967, Montgomery was signed to A&M Records and had seemingly moved over to the more lucrative pop market, although he continued to play hard bop style jazz in small group settings during his live appearances. The three albums released during his A&M period (1967–68), feature Montgomery playing well known pop songs such as Eleanor Rigby using his signature guitar octave technique to render the melody. The A&M recordings were the most commercially successful of his career, although not always well received by critics and fans who preferred his Riverside era.

On the morning of June 15, 1968, while at home in Indianapolis, Montgomery collapsed and died of a heart attack within minutes. He was only 45 years old. Montgomery's home town of Indianapolis later named a park in his honour.

Wes is widely regarded as one of the all-time greats of jazz guitar and is distinctive for his unique approach of playing with his thumb and using octaves and block chord passages in his solos. He is also one of the most imitated jazz guitarists by modern-era players.

Montgomery most regularly played a Gibson L-5 CES guitar. In later years he played one of two L-5 CES guitars Gibson had custom made for him. He used heavy gauge strings on his guitars. For amplification, he variously used Fender Super Reverbs, Standel Super Custom XVs and Twin Reverbs.

Recommended Listening

The Incredible Jazz Guitar of Wes Montgomery

Smokin' at the Half Note

The Wes Montgomery Trio

Wes Montgomery was a master of single-line melody playing and this simple sounding lick really exemplifies his unique melodic approach. A series of quarter note triplets in bars two and three target various chord tones and create tension against the underlying chords. In bar two, the b7, #9 and #5 are all emphasised and imply an altered A7 chord. In bar three, the b7, 9 and 11th are highlighted. In bar four, the 13th is chosen as the target note before the line concludes with the fifth of the Cmaj7 chord in bar five.

For maximum authenticity try playing this example with your thumb in true Wes style.

Example 6a

Octave lines were a major feature of Wes' playing style. Example 6b demonstrates how he used them to fill out the sound of a single line melody. You may need to practise playing scale in octaves to develop your fluency before attempting this example.

As in Example 6a, there is an emphasis on placing chord tones on strong beats. This example adds some chromatic passing notes which helps to make the melody sound stylistically authentic. Notice the use of altered pitches such as the #9 and b9 played over the G7 chord in bar four.

Example 6b

Example 6c returns to single note lines and contains a mixture of rhythmic approaches. Beginning with 1/8th notes and 1/4 note triplets in bar one, longer note durations feature prominently in bars two and three before the more typical 1/8th note bop line in bar four.

Wes used a variety of rhythmic motifs in his playing. Here they are combined with more altered pitches over the dominant 7th chords, especially in bar four.

Take your time with this idea and study the different rhythmic variations. Wes was a master of jazz time and the beginning phrase of this line can be played quite lazily, behind the beat. It's easy to rush phrases with multiple rhythms and ties, so take things slowly at first.

Example 6c

Now we return to octaves and a line with off-beat 1/8th notes that give it forward motion. In this instance the octaves are played primarily on the top E and G strings, or B and D strings, before switching to the G and A strings in the final bar. There is nothing too technically tricky here, it's all about the feel, so pay attention to the timing – especially for the 1/4 triplet in bar three on beats 3 and 4.

Wes used chord extensions (9ths, 11ths and 13ths) a lot in his playing. You can see this in bar three, where the 9th is played against the Dm7 chord on beat 1; also in bar four, where the 9th is played over the G7 chord. The line concludes with the 3rd then the 5th of the Cmaj7 chord.

Example 6d

The final example is another lick in octaves. It uses a number of off-beat 1/8th note rhythms, so be careful with your counting to ensure you play them accurately.

The line begins with a chromatic approach from a half-step above the 5th of the Cmaj7 chord. As in previous examples, there is an emphasis on altered pitches – such as the b9 on the dominant 7th chords in bars two and four.

All the octaves in this lick are played on the top E and G strings, or the B and D strings. Although some players like to use a pick when playing octaves, many adopt Wes' approach and play them with the thumb. The latter generally gives a warmer jazz tone.

Example 6e

7. Barney Kessel

Barney Kessel was born on October 17, 1923 in Muskogee, Oklahoma. He began his musical career whilst still a teenager, touring with local dance bands. At the age of 16 he was playing with an Oklahoma based group called Hal Price & the Varsitonians. To his bandmates he was known affectionately as "Fruitcake" because he practised the guitar almost non-stop, reputedly up to 16 hours a day. He worked with a number of different groups early in his career, including one led by Chico Marx of the Marx Brothers.

In 1944 he appeared in the film *Jammin' the Blues*, alongside Lester Young and also recorded with Charlie Parker's New Stars in 1947 for Dial Records. Quickly gaining a reputation for his musical skills on the guitar, he was rated the No1 guitarist in *Esquire*, *Down Beat*, and *Playboy* magazine polls between the years 1947 and 1960.

By the 1950s, Kessel had made a series of albums called The Poll Winners with bassist Ray Brown and drummer Shelly Manne. Kessel became highly respected for his guitar work in a trio setting, partly because of this trio. He was also the featured guitarist on Julie London's album *Julie Is Her Name* released in 1955. The track *Cry Me a River* from that album (which was a great commercial success), features Kessel playing one of his trademark chordal intro passages. His three Kessel Plays Standards recordings also released in the 1950s feature some of the best playing from this period of his career.

Just prior to Herb Ellis, Kessel was also a member of the pianist Oscar Peterson's trio. He worked with Peterson and bassist Ray Brown for a year before leaving in 1953. Playing guitar with Peterson was considered one of the most challenging gigs for any guitarist at the time, due to Peterson's fondness for fast tempos. Kessel also played and recorded with Sonny Rollins in the late 1950s

By 1957, Kessel's reputation was such that he was offered three signature guitar models by the Kay Musical Instrument Company and, in the early 1960s, Gibson introduced The Barney Kessel model guitar to the market, continuing to make them until 1973. Kessel was regularly winning awards for his musicianship, including *Down Beat* magazine reader's polls in 1956, 1957 and 1958.

By the 1960s, Kessel was a first call session guitarist at Columbia Pictures and became one of the most in-demand recording musicians in America. He is widely regarded a key member of the group of first-call session musicians now commonly referred to as The Wrecking Crew, who played on countless hits in the 1960s, often without their names being listed on the albums they played on.

During the 1970s, Kessel became increasingly involved with music education, presenting his highly popular seminar series "The Effective Guitarist" in various venues around the world. Kessel also performed extensively in a jazz trio with fellow guitarists Herb Ellis and Charlie Byrd, collectively known as The Great Guitars.

Both as a leader or a sideman, Kessel recorded more than 60 albums in his career, primarily with the Verve and Contemporary labels. Kessel was also the musical director of Bob Crosby's TV show, wrote songs and produced records for Ricky Nelson, and played on the soundtracks of feature films such as *Cool Hand Luke*.

Kessel sadly suffered a major stroke in 1992, which effectively ended his musical career. He eventually died of a brain tumour at home in San Diego on May 6, 2004, at the age of 80.

As well as being an inventive and melodic single line soloist, Kessel was widely respected for his expert knowledge of jazz harmony and was an especially skilled chord-melody player, as can be heard in much of his recorded work.

Kessel used a number of signature model guitars in his career, including the Kay K1700, K6700 and K8700, each bearing his signature alongside the Kay logo. He also used a Gibson ES-350 and his signature model made by the same company. He used a variety of amplifiers including the Gibson GA-50T and BR-3 and also played through Polytone amplifiers for a period.

Recommended Listening

Barney Kessel

Kessel Plays Standards Vol 2

The Artistry of Barney Kessel

Barney Kessel's chordal work was amongst the best of his generation and this first example demonstrates his approach over a I VI II V progression in the key of C major. Kessel was an expert at chord substitution and bar one uses Am7 voicings in place of Cmaj7.

In a I VI II V pattern in C major, chord VI would normally be Am7, which jazz players tend to convert to a dominant 7th. In bar two a tritone substitution is used (Eb9) in place of A7. Bar three combines Dm7 and Fmaj7 voicings, the latter being a common substitute for Dm7.

Bar four features another substitution over the G7 chord. Here, an Fm7b5 voicing is used to imply the sound of G7#5b9. The lick ends with a quartal voicing of Em7, substituting for the Cmaj7 chord.

All these substitutions might sound complicated, but if you learn the lick you will hear how effective they are. I suggest playing the straight chord changes a few times, then play the line and you will hear how the substitutions serve to embellish the standard chords.

Example 7a

Example 7b brings together a number of chordal approaches Kessel favoured. In bar one, a Cmaj7 drop 2 voicing is played on beat 2, followed by a short series of diatonic third intervals that lead to the A7#5 chord in bar two. In bar three, a chromatic approach chord of Dbm7 is employed on the up-beat of beat 1 to target the Dm7 chord on beat 2. Approach chords like this are an effective way to enhance your chord solos and accompaniment.

In bar four, two Fm7b5 voicings again suggest a G7#5b9 underneath. The final bar features another Em7 substitution over the Cmaj7 chord, but this is approached from a half-step below (Ebm7). The lick finishes with a slide between two quartal voicings of C major.

You can play this lick fingerstyle or with a pick. Work to make the chord transitions smooth and don't rush the rhythms.

Example 7b

Kessel's single line playing was as sophisticated as his chord work. Example 7c demonstrates his melodic approach over the I VI II V progression. The line begins with an E minor triad over the Cmaj7 chord. In bar two the D Harmonic Minor scale is played over the A7#5 chord, which implies the sound of an A7#5b9.

Jazz guitarists tend to treat dominant chords as though they were V chords. Our chord progression is I VI II V (Cmaj7, A7#5, Dm7, G7) but the A7#5 chord functions as a temporary V7 (often called a secondary dominant), so playing a D minor line over it makes perfect sense.

Bar three contains a simple line drawn from the A Minor Pentatonic scale and is followed by a short sequence of intervals that target the 3rd, #9 and b9 of the G7 chord. Notice how this line eventually resolves to the 3rd and major 7th of the Cmaj7 chord on beat 1 of the last bar. The lick concludes with the major 7th interval again, but played an octave higher.

For rhythmic interest play this line quite straight (not with a heavy swing), as per the audio example. Focus on your timing as it's easy to rush lines like this played at a slower tempo.

Example 7c

The next lick is all about the careful rhythmic placement of chord tones. Two double-stop intervals lead into the 3rd and 5th degrees of the Cmaj7 chord in bar one, beat 1. In bar two, the A7 chord is highlighted by the use of the 3rd and b9 intervals on beat 1, then the 5th and 3rd on beat 3. This two-note interval device, using chord tones, continues in bar three over the Dm7 chord, but the chord tones have now changed to the b3rd and root (beat 1, bar three).

A short series of 5th intervals in bar three provide some melodic contrast before the lick ends with a short scale sequence in bar four. The last 1/16th note of bar four uses a chromatic passing note (Eb) to target the 3rd (E) of the Cmaj7 chord in bar five.

Watch out for the position shifts and slides in this line, especially in bars one and two. Listen to the audio example and notice the slightly behind-the-beat phrasing that helps the line swing.

Example 7d

As with so many jazz guitarists who cut their teeth in a trio setting, Kessel mixed single line melodies with chordal passages when soloing. Example 7e begins with a 1/16th note run from the C Major scale which ends by targeting the root and 5th of the A7 chord in bar two. Notice also the passing note (Ab) on the last beat of bar one.

The scale approach continues with a D Harmonic Minor line played over the A7 chord in bar two. Bar three features a brief rhythmic motif to add variety. The G7 chord in bar four is initially approached by diatonic third intervals before two diminished 7th chords are played on beats 3 and 4. You can use the same fingering for both these chords to help move them from the 6th to 9th position on the fingerboard. The lick finishes with a high register Cmaj7 voicing played on the up-beat of beat 1 in the final bar. Again, don't rush the scale runs in this lick.

Example 7e

8. Jimmy Raney

Often referred to as the "definitive cool jazz guitarist", James Elbert "Jimmy" Raney was born on August 20, 1927 in Louisville, Kentucky. Raney received his first guitar at age 10 and initially studied the instrument with A.J. Giancola, a classical guitar teacher. Another musical mentor, Hayden Causey, helped Raney to begin studying jazz guitar and explore the work of his earliest guitar influence, Charlie Christian.

Hayden Causey also recommended Raney to the Jerry Wald Band in 1944. Jimmy joined the Wald band and remained with them for two months. Al Haig, the pianist from this group, became a significant musical educator for Raney and introduced him to the major bebop players of the period, such as Charlie Parker, Bud Powell and Dizzy Gillespie. Raney began studying the solos of these jazz masters and this helped him form his unique improvisational style.

Raney began his professional musical career in earnest playing in several local groups in the Chicago area. He worked for a time there as the guitarist with the Max Miller Quartet while he was still a teenager, before spending nine months with Woody Herman in 1948. The exposure he gained with Woody Herman led Raney to work with a number of other well-known jazz artists of the period, such as Buddy DeFranco, Artie Shaw and the aforementioned Al Haig, amongst others.

With a growing reputation as a fluid and inventive bop soloist, Raney replaced guitarist Tal Farlow in the Red Norvo group and worked with the bandleader during two periods spanning the early 1950s. Around the same time, he received acclaim for his collaborative work with Stan Getz, and most critics view this musical partnership as amongst his finest work.

Raney spent around six years (1954-1960) working in a diners club with the pianist Jimmy Lyon before returning to work again with Stan Getz in 1962. Despite the high-level work with many jazz stars of the era, Raney had a number of growing health and personal problems (principally alcoholism) and by 1967 had left his base in New York City to return home to Louisville.

Raney returned to music after a hiatus of several years in the early 1970s and began recording albums again. He released a trio album of standards in 1975 (entitled *The Influence*) with bassist Sam Jones and drummer Billy Higgins on the Xanadu label. In 1976 he released another album on the same label featuring over-dubbed guitar duets with himself. The 1979 album *Duets* was a collaboration with his then 22-year old son, Doug Raney, who although clearly influenced by his father, emerged as a fine jazz guitarist in his own right on the recording. The two continued to collaborate into the 1980s and again in the early 1990s.

A little known fact about Raney is that he suffered for many years from Meniere's disease, a degenerative condition that led to significant deafness in both ears. Despite this, the condition did not stop him from playing.

Jimmy Raney died of heart failure in Louisville on May 10, 1995. A fitting obituary in the *New York Times* called him "one of the most gifted and influential post-war jazz guitarists in the world."

Jimmy Raney's playing style was horn-like and his exquisite bebop style lines were always fluently executed and full of swing. Technique never overtook musical taste with Raney and he is one of the most melodic soloists of his generation.

Raney's musical equipment choices remained largely static throughout his career. In the 1970s he played mostly on a Gibson ES-175 through solid-state Polytone amps. On his *Live in Tokyo* record in 1976, he played on his son Doug's Gibson L7 through a Yamaha amp.

Recommended Listening

Live in Tokyo 1976

Nardis (Jimmy and Doug Raney)

But Beautiful

Jimmy Raney's solos were consistently inventive and melodic, and Example 8a demonstrates his signature approach to the first few bars of a popular jazz standard. Bar one begins with a short 1/8th note line which targets the 9th of the Cm7 on beat 3, before resolving to the major third of the F7 chord in bar two.

Bar two features some classic bebop vocabulary. Beginning on beat 3, an F augmented triad is used to resolve to the Bbmaj7 chord that follows. You will hear this idea used frequently in jazz guitar solos.

In bar four, a short 1/8th note line from the Bb Major scale leads into the minor key II – V chords in bars five and six, where the line wraps up with a #9 on the upbeat of beat 2.

This is fairly simple melodic thinking, but is a highly effective approach over fast moving chord changes. As always, play through this line slowly before bringing it up to tempo.

Example 8a

This long bop line demonstrates Raney's ability to use repetitive rhythms to great effect. Bar one has a typical Raney-style line over the Cm7 chord in bar one. The line then targets the major third of the F7 chord on the downbeat of bar two. The doubled 1/8th note motif continues through the next two bars before arriving on the b5th degree of the Am7b5 chord on beat 1 of the last bar.

When considering your own playing, think about how simple rhythmic motifs like this can turn your scale runs into something more engaging for the listener. Aim to emphasise strong chord tones on the downbeats (as in bars three and four, in this case the 3rd of both the Bbmaj7 and Ebmaj7 chords).

Example 8b

Example 8c employs another common bebop technique of combining arpeggios. Bar one begins with a Cm7 arpeggio on beats 1 and 2, with an A diminished arpeggio on beats 3 and 4. Bar two begins with a chromatic passing note before targeting the b9 and #9 on beat 3, and resolving to the major third of the Bbma7 chord.

Bars three and four introduce some rhythmic variety and space. This gives the line some "air" after the flurry of 1/8th notes. (A great tip when creating your own lines is to take a "breath" between phrases. Singing your lines aids this process).

The lick concludes with a three-note figure drawn from the G Harmonic Minor scale – a popular scale choice for the Am7b5 to D7b9 chord change which occurs in this tune.

Example 8c

Raney often used simple, repeated melodic motifs to great effect and Example 8d is a great example of how less can be more. Melodic devices like this help to develop phrasing and are a welcome break from non-stop 1/8th note lines.

Instead of starting on the downbeat of bar one, this 1/16th note motif is played on beat 2 in each bar. Try to use your first and second fingers for the combination of hammer-on/pull-offs required here.

In bar four, the line returns to 1/8th notes with a short scale sequence taken from the Bb Major scale before wrapping up the final bar with a simple three note figure. Note the rhythmic and melodic contrast between the first three bars and the final two in this lick. Balancing rhythmic and melodic phrases like this helps to create a good narrative in your soloing.

Example 8d

Example 8e makes extensive use of rhythmic ties (both within and across the bar lines). Despite the use of 1/8th notes throughout this lick, the addition of the ties helps to create a lot of forward motion to drive the line. If you examine the tied notes, you'll see that they are strong chord tones.

In bars four and five, the rhythmic ties continue and move from the Bb Major scale to the G Harmonic Minor scale in the last bar. Make sure you give each rhythmic tie its full value and refer to the audio to get the timing exact.

Example 8e

9. Joe Pass

Joseph Anthony Jacobi Passalaqua was born on January 13, 1929 in New Brunswick, New Jersey. He was the son of Mariano Passalaqua, a Sicilian immigrant steel worker and was raised in Johnstown, Pennsylvania. Pass received his first instrument (a Harmony model guitar which cost $17) on his 9th birthday. Pass' father quickly realised that his son had a rare musical talent and constantly pushed him to learn songs by ear and to play pieces not written specifically for the guitar, alongside learning various scales and arpeggios. He also encouraged him improvise around the basic melody notes of songs.

Aged just 14, Pass began to get local gigs and was playing with groups led by Tony Pastor and Charlie Barnet, all the time developing his guitar knowledge and understanding of the rigours of the music business. Pass soon began touring with small jazz ensembles and eventually elected to move from Pennsylvania to the more active music scene in New York City.

A few years into his career he developed a serious heroin addiction and, as a result, spent much of the 1950s in prison, away from performing music. Thankfully he managed to overcome his addiction after spending just over two years in a rehabilitation program. Once recovered from his drug habit, he recorded *Sounds of Synanon* in 1962 and it was around this time that he received a Gibson ES-175 guitar as a gift, which he used for touring and recording for many years thereafter.

Pass recorded a number of albums in the 1960s for the Pacific Jazz label, including *Catch Me*, *12-String Guitar*, *For Django* and *Simplicity*. In 1963 he was the recipient of *Down Beat* magazine's New Star Award. Pass also contributed to Pacific Jazz recordings by Gerald Wilson, Bud Shank and Les McCann. Much of Pass' work in 1960s, however, was TV and session work in Los Angeles, working on *The Tonight Show*, *The Merv Griffin Show* and *The Steve Allen Show* amongst others. By the end of the decade, Pass had also worked as a sideman for many popular jazz artists including Frank Sinatra, Sarah Vaughan and Louis Bellson.

By the early 1970s Pass and fellow jazz guitarist Herb Ellis were performing regularly at Donte's jazz club in Los Angeles and this led to the first recording on the new Concord Jazz label. Pass also became involved in jazz education around this period through the publication of several jazz guitar book collaborations, including the highly regarded *Joe Pass Guitar Style* (written with Bill Thrasher).

Pass was later signed to Norman Granz's new Pablo Records label in 1970 and in 1974, Pass released his landmark solo guitar album *Virtuoso* on the same label. In the same year, Pablo Records released the album *The Trio* featuring Pass, pianist Oscar Peterson, and bassist Niels-Henning Ørsted Pedersen. He performed with this trio on many occasions throughout the 1970s and 1980s and the group won a Grammy award in 1975 for Best Jazz Performance.

Whilst working at Pablo Records, Pass also worked with singer Ella Fitzgerald and this became a long-standing collaboration for the duo. They eventually produced six albums together: *Take Love Easy* (1973), *Fitzgerald and Pass...Again* (1976), *Hamburg Duets - 1976* (1976), *Sophisticated Lady* (1975, 1983), *Speak Love* (1983) and *Easy Living* (1986).

Pass continued to record and perform until the early 1990s, sadly passing away in 1994 due to liver cancer in Los Angeles, California, at the age of 65.

Pass was a master of chord-melody and accompaniment and had the uncanny ability to create endless harmonic variations of well-known songs and jazz standards. He was also an exceptional single line bop soloist. His vast knowledge of chord inversions and ability to create improvised basslines and counterpoint is arguably without equal in the jazz world.

Pass mostly played a Gibson ES-175 model during his career, but also played a Fender Jazzmaster when he was recovering from his drug addiction. He also later played guitars by D'Aquisto and Ibanez, who made a signature model for him in the 1980s.

For amplifiers Pass generally used a Polytone, often favouring their Mini-Brute model for its clear jazz tone.

Recommended Listening

For Django

Intercontinental

Virtuoso

Widely respected for his incredible solo chord-melody work, Joe Pass was also an excellent single line bebop soloist. Example 9a demonstrates his ability to play vocal-like melodies over common jazz chord progressions such as the I VI II V I sequence.

In bar one, the 5th and root of the Cmaj7 chord are enclosed by notes a scale step above and semitone below – a common bebop device. In bar two, the augmented fifth of the A7 chord is briefly emphasised on beat 2, then resolved to the natural fifth to suggest an altered dominant sound. In bar three, the fifth of the Dm7 chord is held for two beats before a two-note figure targets the b9 against the G7 in the penultimate bar. Bebop soloists frequently emphasise 3rd and b9 intervals over dominant 7th chords.

When playing this line, notice that while the backing instruments are gently swinging, the first two bars are played straight, which creates a nice rhythmic tension.

Example 9a

Joe Pass often used repeated melodic/rhythmic figures in his single-line soloing as illustrated in Example 9b, which begins with a series of four motifs. When playing this line, make sure to give each beat the correct rhythmic duration (a 1/16th note triplet followed by an 1/8th note). Refer to the audio to hear the exact timing.

In bar two, the 1/16th note triplet approach continues, but only until beat 2 when regular 1/16th notes are used. Bar three is deliberately sparse as a contrast to the busy rhythms of the previous bars. The rhythmic pace picks up again in bar four with a long 1/16th note passage. This line is constructed from the G Altered scale (mode VII of Ab Melodic Minor). Also known as the Super Locrian mode, this is a common device bebop players used to play over dominant 7th chords. The line concludes with the major third of Cmaj7 on beat 1 of the last bar.

Example 9b

No musical examination of Joe Pass's style would be complete without some chord-melody, so Example 9c shows how he often superimposed alternative chords over the original harmony. Like most jazz musicians, Pass rarely stuck to the original chord changes and used a variety of substitutions.

In bar one, two quartal voicings are played on beats 1 and 2, before a conventional Cmaj7 chord on beat 3. A quartal voicing for Em7 is played on beat 4 – a common substitution for Cmaj7.

The chord substitutions continue in bar two with Eb9, A7#5, A7#5#9 and Gm7b5 voicings superimposed over the A7 chord. In effect, they are all altered versions of A7.

Bar three begins with a slide into a quartal voicing of Dm7. A simple two-note phrase leads to a Dm9 voicing at the 10th fret. On beat 4 an Fmaj7 voicing substitutes for Dm7. The penultimate bar substitutes an Fm7b5 voicing for the G7 chord and the line ends with a substituted Em7 chord.

There is a wealth of harmonic information in this example, so work through it slowly at first to understand how and why the substitutions are being used.

Example 9c

This chord melody example begins with a sliding interval approach in 1/8th notes, setting up the Cmaj7 voicing on beat 3 and the quartal voicing on beat 4. Pass often used quartal voicings to enrich the basic harmony of a composition. In bar two, more substitutions are used with a Gm7b5, Eb9 and two diminished 7th chords. Each of these offers a different tension and alteration against the A7 chord.

Some rhythmic variety is added in bar three by an off-beat rhythm on beat 2. In bar four, the same Fm7b5 voicing used in previous examples substitutes for the G7. The lines ends with an Em7 voicing played over the Cmaj7 chord.

Example 9d

The final example of Pass' playing features a long, mainly 1/16th note, line. A double chromatic figure (two consecutive semitones) begins the line before a long chromatic ascent to the beginning of bar three. Over the A7 chord, a series of intervallic sequences are played, all derived from the A Whole Tone scale (another improvisational device Joe Pass used for dominant 7th chords).

In bar three, an Fmaj7 arpeggio on beats 2 and 3 suggest the sound of a Dm9 chord. The penultimate bar uses several altered (chromatic) pitches in 1/16th notes against the G7 chord, including the #5, b9 and #9. The line ends with an octave leap that targets the major third of the Cmaj7 chord. Take your time learning this line and work on it in small sections before putting it all together and bringing it up to tempo.

Example 9e

10. Jim Hall

Born in Buffalo, New York, on December 4, 1930, James Stanley Hall came from a musical household, with his mother, grandfather and uncle all being musicians. Hall began playing the guitar at the age of 10 when his mother gave him an instrument for Christmas. Like many jazz guitarists of his generation, Hall's first influence was the legendary Charlie Christian, but he later became fascinated by horn players such as Coleman Hawkins and Lester Young.

By his teen years, Hall had been living in Cleveland, Ohio, for several years and was already performing with local groups. In his mid-twenties, he decided to study music formally and entered the Cleveland Institute of Music to major in composition and take additional tuition in bass and piano. Later he moved to Los Angeles and continued his studies by taking classical guitar lessons from Vincente Gomez.

In 1956 Hall joined Chico Hamilton's quintet and his career began to take shape professionally. He also worked with the Jimmy Giuffre Three in the 1950s and taught at the Lennox School of Jazz. By 1959 he was working with many of the top names in the jazz world and over the next few years he would collaborate with artists such as Bill Evans, Paul Desmond, Lee Konitz, Sonny Rollins and Ella Fitzgerald.

By the early 1960s, Hall was based in New York and had formed a group with bassist Ron Carter and pianist Tommy Flanagan (the trio was later augmented by the addition of Red Mitchell). He also worked in the house band for the Merv Griffin TV Show, alongside musicians such as Bob Brookmeyer and Art Davis. By this time, Hall was known as a thoughtful and motivic based jazz soloist with rapidly developing compositional and arranging skills.

By the 1970s, Jim Hall was a well-established figure in the jazz world, working not only with jazz musicians but also classical musicians, such as the violinist Itzhak Perlman. His 1975 album with Don Thompson and Terry Clarke (*Jim Hall Live*) is considered one of his finest recordings, along with his duo recordings with pianist Bill Evans and bassist Ron Carter.

Hall continued to record and tour with a variety of groups throughout the 1980s and 1990s and also appeared as a featured soloist with artists such as Michel Petrucciani and Wayne Shorter. Hall hosted the 1990 JVC Jazz Festival in New York and was awarded the New York Jazz Critics Award for Best Composer/Arranger in 1997. His musical collaborations during this period included work with the saxophonist Joe Lovano and also duo concerts with guitarist Pat Metheny (a long-time admirer of Hall's playing).

In recognition of his long career and contribution to jazz music, Hall was awarded an Honorary Doctorate of Music from Berklee College of Music in 1995. His last orchestral composition was a concerto for guitar and orchestra, performed for the first time in June 2004 with the Baltimore Symphony Orchestra. In November 2008, the double album *Hemispheres* was released, featuring fellow guitarist and former student Bill Frisell.

Hall continued to perform regularly into his early 80s and was still appearing at New York clubs and jazz festivals both in the US and Europe. Jim Hall died in his sleep in his apartment in New York in 2013, just six days after his 83rd birthday.

A highly expressive soloist and equally skilled accompanist, Hall's playing for many musicians represented the next evolutionary step in the development of jazz guitar after the players of the bop era. His influence is acknowledged by many contemporary jazz players such as John Scofield, Mike Stern, Mick Goodrick and Pat Metheny.

In the early stages of his career, Hall used a Gibson Les Paul Custom, however he is most closely associated with the Gibson ES-175 guitar. He used this model with a single P90 (single-coil) pickup at first and later a humbucking pickup. He also used a custom D'Aquisto guitar.

For amplification, Hall used a Gibson GA50 amplifier for a period before switching to solid-state combos such as Polytones and Walter Woods amplifiers. Although he generally avoided effects, Hall was known to use a Boss Chorus pedal on occasion.

Recommended Listening

Jim Hall Live

Alone Together (Jim Hall/Ron Carter)

Undercurrent (Jim Hall/Bill Evans)

Jim Hall was a master of melodic phrasing and often used simple motifs to great effect in his soloing. Based on the chord changes to a well-known jazz standard (played here in 3/4 time), observe in this first example how sophisticated phrasing can completely transform a solo.

In bars one and two, a three-note melodic motif is played over the bar line to help create forward motion. The use of space (rests) is crucial here as it gives the melody some "air".

In bar three, off-beat 1/8th note rhythms help to add syncopation before returning to regular 1/4 notes in bar four. In bar six, a short five-note phrase helps target the 3rd of the Cmaj7 chord in bar seven. More off-beat 1/8th notes lead into the scale run in bar eight that concluded with the b3 of the final Cmin7 chord.

When playing this line, notice that every bar has a different rhythm, but still sounds melodic and rhythmically connected.

Example 10a

More rhythmic and melodic motifs feature in Example 10b. The line begins with an F minor arpeggio. Note the rhythmic syncopation here: an 1/8th note followed by two 1/4 notes, then another 1/8th note. Hall emphasised chord tones on the downbeats of each bar.

In bars four and five, the rhythmic phrase from bar one is repeated before an 1/8th note triplet appears on beat 3 in bar six. Bars seven and eight are drawn from the C Major scale and played with consecutive 1/8th notes until the key change in the final bar. There is nothing technically demanding in this lick, but make sure you play accurately the syncopated rhythms in bars one, four and five.

Example 10b

The next example of Hall's style looks simple on paper, but its construction is clever and sophisticated. The line uses mostly chord tones, but the rhythmic phrasing is what makes it interesting. Look at the rhythms used in bars two and three, compared to the other rhythms used in this lick. You'll see that the dotted 1/4 notes used in these two bars divide the bar exactly in half.

This is a popular rhythmic device used by Jim Hall (and many other jazz players) to imply an even time feel (playing in 2) over a 3/4 time signature. Refer to the audio to help you understand the rhythm and its effect against the time signature.

Example 10c

Jim Hall often used intervals of a diatonic second in his playing to create melodic tension against the harmony. At first, they can sound dissonant, but can be effective soloing device if used sparingly with a strong rhythmic construction. The first 4 bars of Example 10d illustrate the approach.

By contrast, the remainder of this lick looks sparse, but uses the dotted 1/4 note rhythm seen in the previous example. Note the use of the b9 interval against the G7 chord on beat 1 of bar six which implies a G7b9 chord, leading nicely to the Cmaj7 chord in bar seven.

Example 10d

Many jazz players use double-stops in their playing and Jim Hall was no exception. This final lick employs some double stops that wouldn't be out of place in Jimi Hendrix's rhythm guitar playing, but work equally well in a straight jazz setting. Beginning in bar one, a series of double stops highlight chord tones for the first four chords until the short bop-style phrase in bar five over the Dbmaj7 chord. The double-stops return in bar seven. Notice how the intervals used here change a little between the various double stops to add some contrast.

This example shows how simple intervals and motifs can help you tell a story with your solo. You don't always have to play long runs of 1/8th and 1/16th notes.

Example 10e

11. Kenny Burrell

Kenneth Earl Burrell was born on July 31, 1931, in Detroit, Michigan. He began playing guitar at the age of 12 encouraged by his parents who were both musicians (his mother played piano and sang and his father played banjo and ukulele). Burrell was initially influenced by both blues and jazz artists including T-Bone Walker, Muddy Waters, Charlie Christian and Django Reinhardt. He began his musical career playing gigs around the Detroit jazz and blues circuit, working with a variety of musicians including pianist Tommy Flanagan and saxophonist Pepper Adams.

Whilst a full-time music student at Wayne State University, he made his recording debut as a member of Dizzy Gillespie's sextet in 1951, followed by the *Rose of Tangier/Ground Round* single which was recorded under his own name at Fortune Records in Detroit. Burrell founded the New World Music Society collective during his college years with fellow Detroit musicians Pepper Adams, Donald Byrd, Elvin Jones, and Yusef Lateef. Burrell also studied privately with classical guitarist Joe Fava. After graduating from Wayne State with a B.A. in Music Composition and Theory in 1955, Burrell toured with pianist Oscar Peterson and then moved to New York in 1956 along with Tommy Flanagan.

Within a few months of arriving in New York, Burrell had recorded his first album as leader for the Blue Note label and both he and Flanagan became highly respected and sought-after sidemen and studio musicians. Over the next few years Burrell worked with many artists including Tony Bennett, Lena Horne, Billie Holiday and Jimmy Smith. Burrell also played with Benny Goodman's band from 1957 to 1959.

Burrell continued recording and performing extensively during the 1960s and '70s. Particularly noteworthy albums include *The Cats* with John Coltrane in 1957, *Midnight Blue* with Stanley Turrentine in 1963, and *Guitar Forms* with legendary jazz arranger Gil Evans in 1965. In 1978, Burrell began teaching a jazz music course at UCLA called Ellingtonia, focusing on the life and works of the great jazz composer Duke Ellington. The two musicians never managed to work with each other directly, but Ellington highly respected Burrell's playing skills and referred to him as his favourite jazz guitarist. Burrell subsequently recorded a number of tributes to and interpretations of Ellington's music.

Burrell continued performing, recording and teaching throughout the 1980s and 1990s, releasing several well-received albums including *Guiding Spirit* (1989), *Sunup to Sundown* (1991), *Collaboration* (1994 with pianist LaMont Johnson) and 1995's *Primal Blue*.

Since 1996, Kenny Burrell has been the Director of Jazz Studies at UCLA (he also founded the program), mentoring a number of notable alumni including Gretchen Parlato and Kamasi Washington. He has also won several jazz polls in Japan and the United Kingdom. Burrell also wrote, arranged, and performed on the 1998 Grammy Award-winning album *Dear Ella* by Dee Dee Bridgewater. In 2004 he received the Jazz Educator of the Year Award from *Down Beat*, and was also named the 2005 NEA Jazz Master.

In 2015, Burrell released a new album called *The Road to Love*, recorded live at Catalina's Jazz Club in Hollywood. This was followed by another live album from the same venue in 2016, where Burrell was accompanied by the Los Angeles Jazz Orchestra.

Burrell's playing is characterised by a unique combination of blues, bebop and classical guitar styles. He switches comfortably between rich chordal passages to swinging, blues-based bop lines with great ease and is a highly sensitive accompanist as well as an inventive soloist.

Burrell has used Gibson guitars for the majority of his career, beginning with ES-175, L-7 and L-5 models. He is, however, most associated with the Gibson Super 400 model and also has a signature model Heritage guitar that is similar in construction to the 400. For amplifiers he used a Fender Deluxe Reverb frequently during the 1950s and later favoured Fender Twin Reverbs. He also occasionally uses Roland JC-120 and Polytone amplifiers.

Recommended Listening

Midnight Blue

The Cats (with John Coltrane)

Blue Bash (with Jimmy Smith)

Kenny Burrell is a master of jazz blues guitar playing and Example 11a demonstrates these skills over a simple three chord vamp. Beginning with a sliding double-stop on the downbeat of bar one, note the use of silence before the bluesy 1/16th note hammer-on and pull-off on beat 4.

Bar two uses a melodic motif following the earlier phrase, alternating between 1/8th notes, 1/16th notes and 1/4 notes before another double-stop at the beginning of the final bar. The double-stops conclude the line on beats 3 and 4.

This whole lick relies on the F Blues scale, but the expert use of rhythm really makes it come alive. It is simple and effective, and this is a masterclass in how to make a jazz blues lick really swing.

Example 11a

Example 11b features another classic Burrell-style lick using a popular blues guitar phrase. The double-stop figure in bar one (beat 2) requires you to let the note on the top E string ring throughout, while you play the hammer-on / pull-off on the B string. Try using your third or fourth finger to fret the top string, while using your first and second fingers for the lower string.

This simple sounding phrase is repeated again in bar two before the lick concludes with another bluesy hammer-on / pull-off phrase. Notice how the line has a "vocal" quality to it. You can create great jazz blues lines from simple phrases.

Example 11b

Example 11c makes effective use of 1/8th note triplets in the opening bar, all based around the common F Blues scale "box position". Ensure that your timing is even here and don't be tempted to rush the phrase, as Burrell plays with a "behind-the-beat" feel. In bar two, the rhythms revert to 1/8th notes and a 1/4 note before the bluesy 1/16th note hammer-on / pull-off figure on beat 4.

The final bar wraps up with a pair of signature Burrell double-stops. There is nothing too demanding here, but it's important to keep the phrase swinging throughout. Try practising this lick with a metronome set to click on beats 2 and 4 and you'll get the swing feel immediately.

Example 11c

The use of a repeated melodic motif or phrase is a trademark of Burrell's guitar playing and this example demonstrates how you can use this approach effectively within a jazz blues solo. Beginning on beat 3 of bar one, the rapid hammer-on / pull-off sequence using the F Blues scale is repeated three times on the top E string before a final 1/8th note triplet run takes the lick to its conclusion.

The rhythmic placement of repeated figures like this is as important as the note choice. Note that the motif didn't start immediately at the beginning of the first bar, but instead arrived on beat 3. This made the motif fall across the bar line between the first and second bars. Learning licks like this will really help to expand and develop your jazz phrasing.

Example 11d

The final Kenny Burrell lick is once more about the effective use of rhythmic placement and a "less is more" approach. Playing a lot of notes is tempting when soloing, but can become tiring for the listener. Listen to the audio for this example to hear just how effective a line can be if its rhythm is carefully constructed. This line could almost be a vocal phrase minus the double stops.

The opening high register double stops in bars one and two are placed quite far apart rhythmically, but still sound musical. A contrast comes in the form of the 1/8th note triplets starting from beat 4 in bar two and continuing into bar three. Incorporating lines like this into your playing will keep you sounding melodic, and keep the audience engaged with your playing.

Example 11e

12. Grant Green

Grant Green was born in St. Louis, Missouri, on June 6, 1935. He was an only child and it was his father who bought him his first guitar, simultaneously introducing him to blues music. Green played a number of different instruments in his early years, including drums and ukulele, before concentrating on guitar. He was mostly self-taught as a guitarist, although he briefly took lessons from a player called Forest Alcorn. His first musical performances were at the age of 13, playing as part of a local gospel ensemble, and around this time he became increasingly interested in jazz music through the recordings of guitarist Charlie Christian and especially horn players such as Charlie Parker.

His first commercial recordings were made in St. Louis with the tenor saxophonist Jimmy Forrest and legendary jazz drummer Elvin Jones for the United record label. In the early 1960s, Lou Donaldson discovered Green playing in a bar in St. Louis and began working with him. Not long after this collaboration began, Green decided to move from St. Louis to New York in 1959.

Through the influence of Lou Donaldson, Green was subsequently introduced to Alfred Lion of Blue Note Records and Lion arranged for him to record as a leader for the prestigious label, although the recording didn't see the light of day until it was eventually released in 2001 as the album *First Session*. Green's recording work for Blue Note was to prove long lasting, and he remained with the label for much of the 1960s, making more recordings, both as a sideman and as a leader, than anyone else signed to the label.

Green's first released album as a bandleader was titled *Grant's First Stand* and was closely followed by the recordings *Green Street* and *Grantstand*. With his reputation rapidly growing, Grant was voted best new star in the *Down Beat* critics' poll in 1962. Whilst signed to Blue Note he also recorded in support of other artists on the label such as Hank Mobley and Stanley Turrentine. Two of his mid-1960s albums, *Idle Moments* (1963, featuring Joe Henderson and Bobby Hutcherson) and *Solid* (1964) are often described as amongst Green's best recordings.

In 1966 Green left the Blue Note label (primarily due to poor earnings) and began recording for other labels, including Verve. Sadly, due to increasing problems with narcotics, the following two years were relatively inactive musically for Green and he also suffered major financial problems. By 1969, however, Green had returned to work with a new funk-influenced group and he went on to record more commercial music. Recordings from this period include the successful *Green is Beautiful* and the soundtrack to the film *The Final Comedown*.

Green's 1970s recordings are of varying quality, although some have since found favour with modern day artists such as US3 and Public Enemy. By the mid-late 1970s Green's health was in serious decline and in 1978 he was hospitalised. Against the advice of his doctors, Green left hospital and went back out on the road as he needed to earn money. While in New York to play an engagement at George Benson's Breezin' Lounge, he collapsed in his car of a heart attack and died on January 31, 1979. He was buried in Greenwood Cemetery in his hometown of St. Louis, Missouri.

Green mostly performed in the hard bop, soul jazz and Latin-influenced idioms throughout his career and commonly in an organ trio setting (a small group featuring organ, drums and guitar).

Aside from guitarist Charlie Christian, Green's primary musical influences were jazz saxophonists, especially Charlie Parker, and his approach was therefore almost exclusively linear rather than chordal. He rarely played traditional rhythm guitar except as a sideman on albums by other musicians.

The simplicity of Green's playing, which tended to avoid the chromatics used by other jazz guitarists, emerged from his early work playing rhythm and blues. Although Green achieved a fusion of this style with bop, he was primarily a blues guitarist and returned almost exclusively to this style of playing later in his career.

Green played a Gibson ES-330 until the mid-1960s, then later a Gibson L7 model with a McCarty pickguard/pick-up. He also played an Epiphone Emperor (with the same pick-up configuration as the L7) and latterly used a custom-built D'Aquisto New Yorker guitar.

According to guitarist George Benson, Grant achieved his signature tone by turning off the bass and treble controls of his amplifier, and turning up the midrange. While he often using whatever amp happened to be setup in the studio he was working in, Green favoured the Fender Tweed Deluxe and Ampeg Gemini combo amplifiers.

Recommended Listening

First Session

Grantstand

Solid

This soulful sounding lick employs the C Blues scale throughout and is mostly played using the popular 8th fret "box" position of the scale. Be sure to add in the indicated slides on beats 2 and 3 in the first bar and keep the triplet beats even throughout. Beginning at the end of bar two (and crossing into bar three) there is a four-note motif which is then rhythmically modified several times. Although played in triplets from beat 3 of bar three, the notes of the motif are actually grouped into fours. Listen to the accompanying audio to hear how this sounds.

The line finishes with a typical bluesy hammer-on / pull-off between the 4th and b5 of the blues scale, before landing on the 5th degree of the Fm chord on beat 1 in the final bar.

Example 12a

Another favourite soloing device of Green's was combining a 1/16th note triplet with an 1/8th note to create a repeating pattern. In bar one, four such motifs are used – one per beat. Make sure you play these evenly and take care not to rush the 1/16th notes. In each case, the 1/8th note at the end of the motif is played on a lower adjacent string. Be careful with the position shifting as well, as you will be moving down the fingerboard to play these patterns from the 10th position to the 8th position.

In bar two, a short four-note phrase in 1/8th notes leads into an Eb Major triad in triplets on beat 4. (Eb Major is the relative major key to C Minor, so a common substitution). The line concludes with the b3 and 5th of the Cm chord on beat 1 of the last bar.

Example 12b

Like many blues influenced jazz players, Green used double-stops in his solos. Examples 12c begins with a series of 1/8th note triplet double-stops that target the 5th and b3 of the underlying Cm chord. Use your first and fourth fingers to play these double-stops and slide into the first triplet note of each beat from a fret below. You'll need to make a small position shift in bar two to play the notes on the 13th and 11th frets on the top E string, and also the first two notes on beat 3, before sliding back down to 8th position for the triplet phrase ending on beat 4 of bar two.

Bar three contains more 1/8th note triplets. Watch out for the rhythm of beat 3 in this bar, where you have to play two 1/16th notes on the middle beat of the triplet. The audio will help you hear the required rhythm. The lick finishes with a simple slide to the 12th fret on the G string and a final Bb note on the 11th fret, B string.

Example 12c

This next example lick begins with an Ebmaj7 arpeggio played over beats 1 and 2. Watch out for the quick slide up to the 13th fret on beat 3, which you should play with either your third or fourth finger, before playing the final triplet on beat 4. Bar two is simpler to finger as it is entirely constructed from the C Minor pentatonic scale in its familiar 8th position shape.

Bar three introduces more Green-style triplet motifs, this time using a mixture of 1/8th and 1/16th notes within a single triplet beat. Motifs like this add structure and form to your soloing and are popular with many jazz guitarists. The lick closes with a simple melodic phrase that mixes dotted 1/8th notes and a triplet. Make sure not to rush the lick and to aim for a relaxed feel in your phrasing as Green used.

Example 12d

Example 12e is another blues-based lick that employs both 1/8th note and 1/16th note triplets. Notice how the 1/16th note triplet figure on beat 3 of bar one is rhythmically displaced in bar two. This helps to create contrast and rhythmic variety. Green often used rhythmic displacement like this to extend motifs across multiple bars.

In bar three, a quick off-beat slide on beat 1 is quickly followed by another combination of 1/16th and 1/8th note triplets, all constructed from the C Blues scale. The lick completes with a series of slides into 1/8th note triplets before targeting the b3 and 4th on beat 1 of the last bar.

Example 12e

61

13. Lenny Breau

Leonard Harold "Lenny" Breau was born on August 5, 1941 in Auburn, Maine, and moved to New Brunswick in Canada when he was just seven years old. Both his parents were musicians performing Country and Western music and Breau began playing guitar at the age of 8. Breau was a gifted player from the start and by his teens was the lead guitarist in the band run by his parents. He was nicknamed "Lone Pine Junior" after his father's stage name of Hal "Lone Pine" Breau. At this point in his musical development, Breau was singing in the band occasionally as well as playing instrumentals by country artists such as Chet Atkins and Merle Travis.

Breau's first recordings were made when he was only 15 years old and were released many years later on the recording *Boy Wonder*. In 1957, the Breau family moved to Winnipeg, Manitoba, and began performing in the region as the CKY family. Some of their performances were broadcast on local radio and around this time Breau's guitar playing came to the attention of Randy Bachman (later the guitarist with *The Guess Who* and *Bachman–Turner Overdrive*).

Becoming more attracted to jazz music, Breau finally left his parent's group in 1959 and began working with local jazz musicians in Winnipeg. He also studied with jazz pianist Bob Erlendson. In 1962, Breau moved to Toronto and formed a jazz group called Three with Eon Henstridge and Don Francks. Breau worked with the group both in Canada and the US, eventually recording a live album in New York. Breau also began to work as a session guitarist, recording for CBC Radio and Television networks. He also hosted his own music program called the Lenny Breau Show on CBS in 1966.

Around this period, Breau's playing came to the attention of the guitarist Chet Atkins who soon formed a friendship with him and two recordings soon appeared on the RCA label, *Guitar Sounds from Lenny Breau* and *The Velvet Touch of Lenny Breau*.

Breau spent much of the next decade moving between different cities in Canada and picking up work wherever he went. He returned to the US in 1976 and once again moved between different cities while continuing to play, compose and also teach guitar. For a period he wrote a popular instructional column in *Guitar Player* magazine. By this point in his career Breau had a loyal following for his unique blend of guitar styles, mixing fingerstyle country guitar techniques with the harmonies of jazz. His use of artificial harmonics inspired many other guitar players to experiment with them.

Despite his otherworldly skills on guitar, Breau struggled with drugs and depression for many years and this affected his career significantly at times, often leaving him with little money and relying on friends for accommodation and support. Despite these problems, Breau produced several solo albums and also collaborated with other musicians, including pedal steel guitarist Buddy Emmons.

After settling in Los Angeles, Breau continued to perform and teach until the early 1980s. With an improvement in his drug related problems, the future looked brighter for Breau until he was tragically found strangled in a swimming pool near his apartment in Los Angeles in 1984. Much mystery surrounds his death, with some speculation that his wife was involved, although she was not charged with his murder.

Breau was posthumously inducted into the Canadian Music Hall of Fame in 1997 and the majority of his albums have been reissued in the years since his death, along with a number of live recordings. At least two documentaries have been made on his life and career since his passing.

Breau's unique playing style amalgamated country, classical, Indian and jazz styles, and his solo arrangements are particularly intricate and piano-like in their construction. His use of a seven string guitar has influenced many players since his death, along with his unequalled mastery of harmonics.

Lenny Breau used a variety of guitars throughout his career, but is probably best known for his use of a seven string guitar. Breau had two custom seven-strings made for him, one classical and one electric. Both these guitars featured a high A string.

Recommended Listening

The Velvet Touch of Lenny Breau: Live!

Five O'clock Bells

Guitar Sounds of Lenny Breau

Lenny Breau's deep understanding of harmony and his ability to craft intricate solo arrangements made him one of the most revered guitar players in jazz. This first example takes a familiar sounding I VI II V progression in C Major and demonstrates a typical approach Breau would use to enrich the basic chord structures.

Breau often used open strings to enhance his chord voicings and the Cmaj9 voicing in bar one uses the open top E string for extra resonance. In bar two, the Am11 chord is fingered in such a way as to allow each note to ring into the next, another favourite Breau technique.

The Dm11 chord voicing in bar three has a small finger slide on the second triplet (play this with your fourth finger) to allow the note to ring against the adjacent G note, played on the top E string at the 3rd fret. A G7#5 chord is used in bar four before the lick concludes with the same Cmaj9 voicing used in bar one. Despite the changes in written time signatures, just try to use your ear to match the audio, as the lick should be played in a rubato fashion.

Example 13a

Arpeggio passages formed a major part of Breau's approach to chord solo arrangements as seen in Example 13b. Although you can use a pick to play this example, fingerstyle or hybrid picking will sound most authentic for Breau's style. The lick begins with a series of three descending arpeggios using quartal chords followed by a drop 2 voicing.

Bar two uses two separate voicings for the G chord. Note the use of open strings in the rich sounding G13b9 voicing. Bar three uses the Cmaj9 voicing from the previous (again with the open top E string) before another quartal voicing appears in bar four. This voicing, (Em11) is played twice, the second time with artificial harmonics.

Artificial harmonics are sounded by playing a "mirror-image" of the chord voicing you are holding, 12 frets above the original shape. It can be tricky to play cleanly and Breau was a recognised master of this technique. He generally played these harmonics using his right hand thumb to pluck the string behind his index finger, which lightly touched the fret exactly 12 frets above the fingered chord shape.

Example 13b

Example 13c is entirely played with artificial harmonics using the technique described above. Beginning with the Gmaj7 chord voicing in bar one, play the harmonics exactly 12 frets higher than the original chord shape (on the same strings) and you should get the desired result. It sometimes takes a bit of effort to achieve a clear ringing tone, but you should soon be able to achieve this with concentrated practise. Fingers are definitely recommended here, rather than a pick.

The artificial harmonics are played through each of the different chord voicings in order: Bb13, Am11, Ab7b5 and Gmaj7. Take your time with these voicings and perhaps play them without the harmonics to begin with, to practise moving between the chord shapes comfortably. (The Ab7b5 chord is actually a chord substitution for D7 – a tritone substitution).

Example 13c

The next lick might sound as though it belongs in a book on Country guitar playing, but Breau would often use double-stop licks like this, especially when playing a blues. He was a great fan of Chet Atkins and Jerry Reed, both of whom had a strong country influence in their playing.

The lick utilises double stops throughout and shifts between 3rd and 5th position. Play the quick triplet figure in bar one (beat 2) using your fourth, third and index fingers to cover the two required strings (the G and B strings). This will help you execute the phrase comfortably. Remember to slide up to the double-stop played on the up-beat of beat 4 in bar one. The lick finishes on a G13 voicing and would work well within a G blues progression.

Example 13d

Many of Lenny Breau's solo arrangements used lush sounding chord voicings incorporating open strings – especially during introductions and endings. This final example uses an Em9 voicing in bar one, with three open strings added (the low E, G and high E strings). Make sure you let each string ring into the next, which will create a harp-like effect.

In bar two, the chord form from bar one is modified by raising one note (the 5th degree) to create an Em9#5 chord, before returning to the original voicing. In bar four, an open-sounding Aadd9 voicing (again using three open strings) is played. The same voicing is played a second time using artificial harmonics. Use the same technique described above to play the harmonics and let all the notes in each chord ring for as long as possible.

Example 13e

14. John McLaughlin

John McLaughlin was born on 4 January 1942 in Doncaster, South Yorkshire, and began playing guitar when he was around 11 years old. He was brought up in a musical environment as his mother was a concert violinist and he studied both the piano and violin before switching to guitar. McLaughlin was initially attracted to blues and swing music and after moving to London in the early 1960s, he worked with artists such as Alexis Korner, Graham Bond, Brian Auger and Georgie Fame. He also supported himself with a variety of session work in London and gave guitar lessons to future Led Zeppelin guitarist Jimmy Page.

In January 1969, McLaughlin recorded his debut album *Extrapolation* featuring John Surman on saxophone and Tony Oxley on drums. McLaughlin thereafter moved to the US to join drummer Tony Williams' group *Lifetime*. He also met and jammed with rock guitar legend Jimi Hendrix the same year. He subsequently played with trumpeter Miles Davis on several jazz–rock albums including *In a Silent Way*, *Bitches Brew*, *Live-Evil*, *On the Corner*, *Big Fun* and *A Tribute to Jack Johnson*. McLaughlin also worked as a sideman with other well-known jazz artists of the era, such as Miroslav Vitous, Larry Coryell, Wayne Shorter and Carla Bley.

McLaughlin's 1970s electric band, The Mahavishnu Orchestra, included violinist Jerry Goodman, keyboardist Jan Hammer, bassist Rick Laird and drummer Billy Cobham. They performed a highly complex style of music that fused jazz and rock with Eastern and Indian music. The Mahavishnu Orchestra sadly suffered from personality clashes and the group split in late 1973 after two years and three ground-breaking fusion albums. McLaughlin reformed the group several times in the 1970s with different line-ups.

McLaughlin then became heavily involved in acoustic playing with his Indian classical music based group Shakti. The group recorded three albums: *Shakti* (1975), *A Handful of Beauty* (1976) and *Natural Elements* (1977).The band introduced ragas and Indian percussion to the jazz world.

In 1979 McLaughlin joined up with flamenco virtuoso Paco de Lucía and jazz guitarist Larry Coryell (replaced by Al Di Meola in the early 1980s) to form the all-acoustic Guitar Trio. The Trio reunited in 1996 for a second recording session and a world tour. In 1979 McLaughlin also recorded the album *Johnny McLaughlin: Electric Guitarist*, a return to mainstream jazz/rock fusion and the electric guitar.

In the 1980s McLaughlin formed The One Truth Band and recorded one studio album, *Electric Dreams*, with L. Shankar on violins, Stu Goldberg on keyboards, Fernando Saunders on electric bass and Tony Smith on drums. In 1981 and 1982, McLaughlin recorded two further albums, *Belo Horizonte* and *Music Spoken Here* with The Translators – a group of French and American musicians. From 1984 to 1987, McLaughlin worked with a quintet simply titled Mahavishnu recording two albums: *Mahavishnu* and *Adventures in Radioland*. Alongside this Mahavishnu project, McLaughlin also worked in a duo format with bassist Jonas Hellborg.

In 1986 he appeared with Dexter Gordon in Bertrand Tavernier's film *Round Midnight*. He also composed *The Mediterranean Concerto*, which was orchestrated by Michael Gibbs. McLaughlin released a Bill Evans tribute album in 1993 entitled *Time Remembered: John McLaughlin Plays Bill Evans*.

In 2003 he recorded a ballet score, *Thieves and Poets*, and a three-DVD instructional video on improvisation entitled *This is the Way I Do It*. In June 2006 he released the album *Industrial Zen*, on which he experimented with the Godin Glissentar.

In 2007 McLaughlin left Universal Records, joined the Abstract Logix label, and began touring with a new jazz fusion quartet, The 4th Dimension, consisting of keyboardist/drummer Gary Husband, bassist Hadrian Feraud and drummer Mark Mondesir. In recent years, McLaughlin has toured with Remember Shakti amongst others and in 2017 undertook a retirement tour in the US announcing that in 2018 he would not be touring again, but instead just performing selected engagements.

McLaughlin is a Grammy award winner and has been awarded multiple Guitarist of the Year and Best Jazz Guitarist awards from publications such as *Down Beat* and *Guitar Player* magazine.

McLaughlin's guitar style incorporates speed, high technical precision and great harmonic sophistication. He is widely known for using non-Western scales and odd or unconventional time signatures. Indian music has also had a profound influence on his guitar style.

John McLaughlin has used many guitars over his career including several double-necked guitars and the first Abraham Wechter-built acoustic, the Shakti guitar. He has also used a Godin and a Gibson Brydland. In recent years he has used a PRS model guitar.

McLaughlin has used a variety of amplifiers in his career including Marshall 100watt amps, but more recently he has plugged into a preamp instead of a regular amplifier, then run the signal direct into the PA system of the venue.

Recommended Listening

Shakti (John McLaughlin with Shakti)

Johnny McLaughlin: Electric Guitarist

Visions of the Emerald Beyond (Mahavishnu Orchestra)

John McLaughlin's formidable alternate picking technique and extensive harmonic knowledge enable him to execute fast scale passages, even over the most complex chord changes. The following example demonstrates how McLaughlin might approach the first few bars of a well-known John Coltrane composition.

McLaughlin solos often feature long scale passages of 1/16th notes, as seen here. Beginning in bar one, the chord scales shift from B major to G major on beat 3, and then in bar two to Eb major on beat 3. Note the use of a chromatic passing tone in the 1/16th note passage on beat 2 of bar two, which helps to arrive at the G note on the 8th fret, B string. The line also features a Bb arpeggio on beats 3 and 4 of the final bar.

With a high velocity line like this, start slow and bring it up to tempo gradually with the assistance of a metronome.

Example 14a

McLaughlin uses a lot of pentatonic patterns and short melodic scale sequences/motifs in his playing (likely influenced by saxophonists such as John Coltrane). Example 14b displays this approach in action. Bar one uses sequences drawn from the B Major scale on beats 1 and 2, which then resolve to the G Major scale for the remaining two beats of the bar.

In bar two, the four-note sequences on beats 3 and 4 are now derived from the C Minor Pentatonic scale and continue into bar three using the same scale. This scale application is then lowered by a half step in bar four to the B Minor Pentatonic scale to accommodate the key change to G Major. The lick concludes on the 5th degree of the Gmaj7 chord in the final bar. Whilst pentatonic scales are often viewed as the territory of rock and blues guitarists, McLaughlin's playing shows that they can work effectively over complex jazz harmony.

Example 14b

More rapid scale transitions are evident in Example 14c, but this time with a combination of 1/16th note and 1/8th note rhythms. The first two beats in bar one ascend a B Major scale in 1/16th notes, then resolve to the first available scale tone in G Major on beat 3. These seamless scale connections are a feature of McLaughlin's playing and give great fluidity to his lines.

In bar two (beat 3) combined 1/8th and 1/16th note rhythms give some variety to the Eb Major scale, before a five-note motif in bar three concludes the lick. To emulate McLaughlin's scale mastery, try shifting to the nearest available tone in each new scale when you improvise. You'll find that this approach sounds melodic, especially over multiple chord/key changes.

Example 14c

Example 14d is a pentatonic scale workout showing how you can use five-note scales over multiple key changes and still remain true to the harmony. In bar one, a C# Minor Pentatonic scale is played over the Bmaj7 chord on the first two beats. Then, to accommodate the first key change (to D7 on beat 3) the scale changes to B Minor Pentatonic.

In bar three, when the Bb7 chord appears, the C Minor Pentatonic scale comes into play and remains in operation until the last note of the lick on beat 1 in the final bar. The lick only uses these three minor pentatonic scales: C# Minor, B Minor and C Minor, but they work effectively against the underlying harmony.

Example 14d

The final McLaughlin lick is also based on minor pentatonic scales. Beginning with G# Minor Pentatonic over the Bmaj7 chord in bar one, it switches to A Minor Pentatonic for the D7 chord. As in the previous example, the C Minor Pentatonic scale is played beginning on the Bb7 chord and continuing to bar four, where the key change necessitates switching to B Minor Pentatonic.

While McLaughlin obviously uses many melodic devices and scales in his playing, his mastery of pentatonic scales is second to none, and studying some of his lines will really enhance your soloing skills.

Example 14e

15. George Benson

George Benson was born on March 22, 1943 and raised in the Hill District of Pittsburgh, Pennsylvania. By the tender age of just 7, he was playing the ukulele in a corner store. By the age of 8, he was playing guitar in an unlicensed nightclub on Friday and Saturday nights. Something of a child prodigy, Benson was already recording by the age of 9 and released *She Makes Me Mad* and *It Should Have Been Me*, on the RCA-Victor label in New York.

Amongst Benson's early influences on guitar were the country jazz guitarist Hank Garland and swing jazz great Charlie Christian. His first steps in the music industry apparently had an adverse effect on his schoolwork and because of this his guitar was impounded! After some time in a juvenile detention centre, however, he was made a new guitar by his stepfather and resumed playing.

Benson then attended Schenley High School and upon graduation began working with the organist Jack McDuff, playing predominantly instrumental soul jazz. At the age of 21, Benson recorded his debut album as a leader, *The New Boss Guitar*, which also featured McDuff on organ. His next recording was titled *It's Uptown* (with the George Benson Quartet) and this time included Lonnie Smith on organ. This album was followed by *The George Benson Cookbook*, once more with Lonnie Smith and also Ronnie Cuber on baritone saxophone.

By this time, Benson's highly distinctive jazz-blues guitar style was gaining considerable attention from his fellow musicians, and he was subsequently hired by the legendary Miles Davis to play on the track *Paraphernalia* from Davis' 1968 recording, *Miles in the Sky*.

Benson then signed with jazz label CTI Records, recording several commercially successful jazz albums including *Bad Benson*, *Good King Bad* and *Benson and Farrell* (with Joe Farrell). Benson also recorded a version of The Beatles Abbey Road album entitled *The Other Side of Abbey Road* and a version of *White Rabbit*, most notably recorded by Jefferson Airplane. He also found time to play on sessions for other artists signed to CTI, including Freddie Hubbard and Stanley Turrentine.

By the late 1970s, Benson was recording for the Warner Brothers label and also now singing regularly on his recordings, which he had only done infrequently until this point. His 1976 release, *Breezin'*, featured his lead vocal on the track *This Masquerade*, which was a huge hit in the pop charts and won him a Grammy Award for Record of the Year. The album also included a cover of the Jose Feliciano composition *Affirmation*. *Breezin'* was successful for Benson and became his bestselling work to date, despite the record company initially being reluctant for him to sing rather than just play guitar.

George Benson also recorded the original version of the song *The Greatest Love of All* for a 1977 biographical film about boxer Muhammad Ali (called *The Greatest*). Around this period Benson recorded with the German conductor Claus Ogerman and worked with trumpeter Freddie Hubbard on a number of his albums throughout the 1960s, 1970s and 1980s.

More commercial success followed and a live recording of the track *On Broadway* won Benson a Grammy award in 1978. His breakthrough pop album was *Give Me The Night* (1981) produced by Quincy Jones and in subsequent years he has had many hit singles such as *Love All the Hurt Away*, *Turn Your Love Around*, *Lady Love Me* and *20/20*.

In 1990, Benson was awarded an Honorary Doctorate of Music from the Berklee College of Music and was also recognised as a Jazz Master by the National Endowment of the Arts.

In more recent years, Benson has also released the album *Guitar Man*, which revisits his 1960s and early-1970s guitar playing style on an album of jazz and pop standards. Now well into his seventh decade, George

Benson still records and performs from his extensive musical back catalogue and is widely regarded as one of the great jazz guitarists.

Benson's fluid and highly inventive soloing style mixes blues, soul and mainstream jazz in a unique way that few other players have achieved. His use of octaves and intervals is especially inventive and whilst influenced by players like Wes Montgomery, his sound and improvisational approach are instantly identifiable as his own.

Benson has long been associated with Ibanez guitars and the company have produced a number of signature models bearing his name including the LGB300. Earlier in his career he also used a Gibson L-5 CES as played by Wes Montgomery.

For amplification, he has been most recently been using a Fender George Benson Hot Rod Deluxe or Twin Reverb amplifier, usually without any guitar effects or signal processing.

Recommended Listening

The George Benson Cookbook

It's Uptown

Breezin'

Guitar Man

George Benson's soloing style is instantly identifiable and mixes intricate bebop lines with fast blues runs and octave passages, reminiscent of Wes Montgomery. Benson also creates melodic ideas from simple double-stops, as seen in this first example.

In bar one, a double-stop slide targets the 9th and 11th of the Dmaj9 chord. In harmonic situations like this, however, Benson often "thinks" of the V chord related to the major chord, so here he is thinking of an A7 (V chord in the key of D Major). The A7 substitution approach continues with a familiar bluesy double-stop phrase which is repeated in bar two. Notice how the rhythmic placement changes slightly between these otherwise similar phrases.

The double-stop intervals return in the last bar, but this time played as 1/4 note triplets. Try to keep these double-stops on the same string pair, as this helps with the position shifting required in this lick.

Example 15a

The A7 substitution approach is also evident in this second lick. It begins with an A Major Pentatonic phrase that leads into bar one and continues until the short bend at the beginning of bar two. Benson doesn't bend strings particularly high in pitch, and this is characteristic of the small blues bends he uses from time to time.

Beginning in bar three, there is a chromatic ascent from the 8th fret on the top E string to the 12th fret, before an A Major triad is outlined at the end of beat 3 going into beat 4. Be careful to get the rhythms accurate here and refer to the audio for the exact timing. This is a typical Benson move which introduces a great blues feel to the line. The lick concludes with an A Major triad in the final bar played over the underlying G/A chord.

Example 15b

Benson is a master of using chromatic passing notes in his solos and Example 15c is a typical example of this. Beginning with a chromatic run up to the first 1/16th note of bar one, the same sequence of notes is then reversed before playing the B note on the 12 fret on beat 2. A quick fingering shift from the 9th position down to the 5th is then required on beat 3 of bar one to complete the rest of the bar.

More chromatic passing notes on beat 4 of bar one lead into the bluesy sounding 1/16th note passage in bar two. The lick finishes with a typical Benson double-stop figure in bar three. Longer lines like this often take some extended practice to sound really fluent, so do learn this in small sections at first. Don't worry about speed until you can execute the line accurately at a slow tempo.

Example 15c

Example 15d looks deceptively simple on paper, but is musically effective against the backing harmony. Using the interval of a fifth, the sliding double stops in bar one initially target the sixth and major seventh of the

Dmaj9 chord and, quickly thereafter, the fifth and ninth. The long sequence of quarter note triplets beginning on beat 3 of bar two use a favourite Benson technique: playing an octave fingering, but adding a scale pitch within the octave interval.

In this example, the interval added to the octave is the fourth (15th fret on the B string) giving a shape that is built: root, 4th, octave. Provided you restrict this shape to notes contained within the chord / scale you are playing, you can move this three-note figure around the fretboard to great effect.

Example 15d

The final George Benson lick returns to the A7 substitution approach discussed earlier and features a long 1/16th note line. Some quick position shifting is required from the pickup run leading into the first beat of bar one, so practise this slowly until you can play it automatically. The long run beginning on beat 4 of bar one is played in 8th position, before you have to move down to 5th position for the last two 1/16th notes of bar two. Note the use of the chromatic passing notes throughout this long line.

In bar three there is another chromatic climb beginning halfway through the first beat, which goes up the 9th fret on the G string. The line finishes back at 5th position and with more chromatic notes leading to the repeated A note in the final bar. Once again, master this line at a slower tempo before speeding up.

Example 15e

16. Pat Martino

Born Pat Azzara on August 25, 1944 in Philadelphia, Pennsylvania, Pat Martino began playing guitar around the age of 12. His father, Carmen "Mickey" Azzara was a local club singer and jazz fan who exposed the young Martino to jazz from an early age. Martino left school in tenth grade to devote himself to music and then studied with Dennis Sandole, who also taught John Coltrane. Martino was initially influenced by jazz guitarists such as Wes Montgomery and Johnny Smith.

Martino began playing professionally at the tender age of 15 after moving to New York City, where he was soon playing at noted jazz clubs such as Smalls Paradise. He later moved into a suite in the President Hotel on 48th Street to be near the clubs he was playing in. He would play at Smalls for six months of the year, and then in the summer months play at the Club Harlem in Atlantic City. Martino's reputation quickly grew and he became a much sought-after sideman and soloist, especially in the organ trios of players like Jack McDuff and Don Patterson. He also became heavily immersed in the emerging soul-jazz scene in New York.

When Martino was just twenty he was signed as a leader to Prestige Records and produced a series of albums for the label including, *El Hombre*, *Strings* and *Desperado*. His 1972 album *Pat Martino Live* features an extended solo on the song *Sunny*, which remains one of his most celebrated solos and is an excellent example of his long 1/16th note lines, mixed with repeated rhythmic motifs. Martino's distinctive soloing style and incredibly fluid improvisations gathered a loyal fan following during the early to mid-1970s and he continued touring and recording until 1976 when he began experiencing severe headaches, which grew worse until he was diagnosed with a brain aneurysm.

Martino had been performing constantly up until the aneurysm suddenly left him with severe amnesia, giving him no recollection or knowledge of his previous career. Perhaps even more worrisome for his career, he also had no knowledge of the guitar or how he had previously played the instrument. After surgery and a lengthy recuperation period, Martino had to virtually learn the guitar from scratch again and didn't finally return to performing until 1987 with the release of the appropriately titled album *The Return*. Following this comeback recording, he again took a hiatus when his parents became ill and it was not until 1994 when he recorded the albums *Interchange* and *The Maker* that he returned to music full time.

Having overcome huge personal obstacles in his career, Martino is now back performing regularly and recording. He is deeply thoughtful and philosophical with regard his approach to jazz music and this is reflected in both his compositional approach and his playing and teaching.

Martino has received many accolades and awards in his career including Guitar Player of the Year in the *Down Beat* magazine Readers' Poll of 2004, two Grammy Award nominations in 2002 for Best Jazz Instrumental Album (*Live at Yoshi's*) and Best Jazz Instrumental Solo on *All Blues*. In 2003 he received Grammy nominations for Best Jazz Instrumental Album with *Think Tank* and Best Jazz Instrumental Solo on *Africa.*

Pat Martino has also released several instructional videos and books covering his unique approach to jazz improvisation. He continues to record and perform live and his last album, *Formidable,* was released in 2017.

Martino's musical approach is much in the hard-bop jazz genre, but also incorporates elements from World music and even rock. His long, rapid-fire 1/16th note passages are much emulated by other guitarists, although few achieve his level of fluency and inventiveness.

Martino has used a variety of guitars throughout his long career, including a Benedetto Signature guitar (his current instrument), a PM Gibson signature model, and various other Gibson models including a Les Paul Custom and L-5. He uses heavy gauge strings and picks. For amplifiers he has used Fender Twin Reverbs and Roland JC-120s, but in recent years has favoured an Acoustic Clarus Head played into a Mesa Boogie cabinet.

Recommended Listening

Pat Martino – Live

El Hombre

Remember: A Tribute to Wes Montgomery

Beginning with a bluesy double-stop, this rather simple sounding lick demonstrates Martino's ability to superimpose lines built from an alternative chord to the one being played over. Here the original chord is Dm9, but the line suggests more of a G7 sound. Note the emphasis on the note B (the major 3rd of G7), seen in bar two (beat 3) and bar three (beats 1 and 2). This type of "on-the-fly" chord substitution is common in Martino's playing.

Pat Martino generally uses heavy strings and a thick pick to achieve his dark, expressive sound, so you may want to try and move up a string gauge to emulate that if possible.

Example 16a

Martino favours 1/16th note runs in his improvisation and Example 16b employs this rhythmic approach to great effect. Beginning with a 1/16th note triplet figure on the top E string, the line descends rapidly using what has been termed the Bebop Dominant scale. This is a regular Mixolydian mode with an added major 7th degree.

As with the previous example, the thinking here is based around a G7 chord rather than the Dm9 played in the backing track. Take your time building this line up to full tempo.

Example 16b

More substitutions are evident in this next 1/16th note example, which begins with an Fmaj7 arpeggio in the 7th position. Fmaj7 superimposed over Dm7 creates a Dm9 sound, so this is a effective chord substitution and a Martino favourite. There is a chromatic passing note employed on the last 1/16th note of beat 2 in the first bar and again on beat 3 in the same bar.

Martino uses such passing notes to ensure his lines have some chromatic "colour" and also to help him land on chord tones on the stronger beats in each bar. In bar two the G Bebop Dominant scale is in use once more.

Example 16c

Beginning with a brief Emin7 arpeggio on beat 1 in the first bar, this busy sounding lick features a more involved use of chromatic passing notes. Passing notes are used cleverly to target the notes of a G Major triad. Bar two uses a highly chromatic scale ascent up to a high D note on the 10th fret on the top E string, before finishing with a bluesy double-stop in the final bar.

With these long 1/16th note lines, make sure you don't rush the phrasing and keep steady time throughout. You may also need to work a little more on your alternate picking technique to get these up to full tempo.

Example 16d

The final Pat Martino lick is full of the techniques seen in the earlier examples and begins with a double chromatic approach (two consecutive semitones) that descend to the b7 of the Dm9 chord. Bar one has several chromatic passing notes before the more diatonic melody at the beginning of bar two. The chromatic notes return again by the last beat of bar two and continue until the final bar, giving the whole line a hard-bop jazz flavour that is classic Martino.

When learning longer lines such as this, break them down into smaller sections, rather than trying to learn them all at once. You may need to slightly adapt your regular scale fingerings to achieve fluency when using multiple passing notes.

Example 16e

17. Larry Carlton

Larry Eugene Carlton was born in March, 1948 in Torrance, California. He began studying guitar at the early age of 6 and soon became interested in jazz through listening to legendary guitar players such as Joe Pass, Barney Kessel and Wes Montgomery. He was also attracted to the music and blues guitar playing of B.B. King. He attended junior college and Long Beach State College while playing professionally at clubs in and around the Los Angeles area.

Carlton's rapidly developing playing expertise and background in both jazz and rock/pop music made him a rising star within the Los Angeles session scene of the 1970s. Eventually playing on hundreds of recording sessions and movie soundtracks, he was equally at home with pop, jazz, rock and even country record dates, making him a highly sought after studio guitarist. His work with Steely Dan and with Joni Mitchell drew much critical praise and his legendary solo on *Kid Charlemagne* by Steely Dan is considered one of the finest recorded guitar solos of all time, as ranked by *Rolling Stone* magazine. He worked with virtually every major record producer from the 1970s and 80s and his musical versatility saw him appear on over 100 gold records.

Alongside his session work, Carlton has also had a long running solo career beginning with his 1968 debut album *With A Little Help From My Friends*. In the mid-70s he built a home studio and called it Room 335 after the Gibson ES-335 model guitar he'd played for many years as his main instrument. He has recorded most of his albums at Room 335 and one of his best-known compositions is also named after the studio. Carlton produced six solo albums from 1978 to 1984 and had some notable commercial success with his version of Santo Farina's track *Sleepwalk*. He was also a member of the jazz fusion group The Crusaders and in 1981 he received a Grammy Award for Best Pop Instrumental Performance for the theme from the popular US TV series *Hill Street Blues*. Carlton also produced a live album called *Last Nite* in 1986.

In 1988, with his solo career progressing strongly, he was shot in the throat by a teenager outside the Room 335 studio and suffered nerve and vocal cord damage, which delayed the completion of the album he was working on at the time, *On Solid Ground*. His left arm was paralyzed and for six months he was unable to play properly. Thankfully, he recovered after this incident and has gone on to record more solo albums and has worked with the group *Fourplay* amongst others.

In more recent years, Carlton has collaborated with fellow studio guitarists Lee Ritenour and Steve Lukather and he was also commissioned to compose music for the king of Thailand, Bhumibol Adulyadej, in honour of the king's birthday. Carltons' other musical awards include a Grammy Award for Best Pop Instrumental Performance for *Minute by Minute* in 1987, and further Grammy Awards for Best Pop Instrumental Album, *No Substitutions: Live in Osaka* in 2001 and Best Pop Instrumental Album, *Take Your Pick* in 2010.

Carlton's highly distinctive playing style mixes bebop jazz lines with an almost pedal-steel like string bending approach. His use of mixed triads in his solos contrasts with many of the more scale orientated players of his generation. An inventive, melodic and highly expressive soloist, many artists have taken advantage of his distinct playing style to complement their music.

Carlton is probably best known for his use of a 1969 Gibson ES-335 guitar. In fact, he gained the nickname "Mr 335" for his use of this particular instrument, which became a mainstay of the LA studio guitar scene in the 1970s and '80s. Other guitars he has owned and played include a 1951 Fender Telecaster, a 1964 Fender Stratocaster, and a 1955 Gibson Les Paul Special.

For amplifiers he has used a Fender Vibrolux and Princeton, but his standard setup generally includes a Dumble amplifier, made by legendary amp designer Howard Dumble. Carlton uses effects sparingly in his playing, but does employ some delay and reverb on his signature guitar sound.

Recommended Listening

Larry Carlton

Last Nite

The Royal Scam (Steely Dan)

Example 17a begins with a G Major Pentatonic line in 5th position and works its way up the neck to the 10th position using two positional slides on the D and G strings. In bar two, bend the B string up a whole step to the 12th fret, then use your fourth finger to play the high D note on the top E string at the 10th fret.

In bar three, bend and release the B string as indicated at the 10th fret. A short pentatonic phrase follows in 8th position. The typical Carlton phrase in bar four emphasises the 3rd of the underlying D7 chord, and the lick finishes with the minor 3rd of Cm7 to highlight the key change in bar five.

To get the Carlton sound, use a slightly overdriven guitar tone to give you some sustain and maybe add some compression.

Example 17a

Starting with a 1/16th note pickup phrase in 5th position, play the half-step bend on the high E string in bar one and make sure you arrive at the 7th fret on the B string at the beginning of bar two and add vibrato to the note. Larry Carlton often uses these simple sounding bends and melodies to outline the chord changes. Notice how he uses chord tones at the beginning of each bar.

Staying in 5th position, the lick uses the A Dorian mode for bars three and four, with chord tones again falling on the first beat of each bar. Pay particular attention to the timing of the 1/4 note triplet on beats 3 and 4 in bar four.

Example 17b

Beginning with a short 1/8th note lead-in melody, Example 17c is classic Larry Carlton, using super-accurate string bends to outline the harmony. In bar three, bend up a whole-step on the high E string and be sure to give the note its full rhythmic duration before releasing it back down. In bar three, watch out for the half-step bends and try to let each of the strings ring into each other – a major feature of Carlton's style.

The short melody and half-step bend in bar five demonstrates how deftly Carlton handles key changes. Make sure you refer to the audio to get the timing correct on this final phrase.

Example 17c

There are more half-step bends in this blues-inspired lick which uses the A Dorian mode for the scale passages. The lick begins with a high register bend up at the 15th fret. In bar two there is a scale descent down the A Dorian mode. Notice how Carlton regularly mixes long bends and simple sounding scale passages to create his signature melodic sound.

In bar four there are two 1/4 note triplets before the final long bend in bar five. Make sure you give this bend its full rhythmic duration before playing the final note on the 8th fret, B string, and adding some vibrato. Make sure you avoid rushing this example and keep your timing even and accurate throughout.

Example 17d

The final example lick begins with a 1/16th note lead-in to the held D note at the 10th fret on the top E string. Make sure you add some vibrato here to give a singing quality to the note. Achieving this vocal quality is another big feature of Carlton's playing. More string bends follow moving into bar two. Watch out for the half step bend targeting the seventh of the Am7 chord on beat 1 in bar three.

The A Dorian mode is used once more for the scale passages in the remainder of bar three and also in bar four before the lick concludes with the flat seventh and minor third of the Cm7, marking the key change to Bb Major.

Example 17e

18. John Scofield

John Scofield was born on December 26, 1951 in Dayton, Ohio, and was raised in rural Connecticut. Originally inspired by both blues and rock players, Scofield began playing guitar when he was 11 years old and his interest in music continued to develop through his high school years, until he decided to enrol at the Berklee College of Music in Boston in 1970. Whilst studying at Berklee, Scofield began to make a name for himself playing locally in the Boston area and upon leaving the college he recorded with Gerry Mulligan and Chet Baker.

Scofield then toured and recorded with fusion drummer Billy Cobham and keyboardist George Duke for a period of two years and worked with Gary Burton and Charles Mingus. In 1976, Scofield signed with Enja Records and the following year released his first solo album called simply *John Scofield*. In 1978 he recorded the landmark album *Rough House* featuring pianist Hal Galper and he went on to work with Galper again on the musician's album *Ivory Forest*.

Scofield formed a new trio in 1979 with drummer Adam Nussbaum and bassist Steve Swallow and by 1982 he was working with the legendary jazz trumpeter Miles Davis. He played with Davis on the albums *Star People*, *Decoy* and *You're Under Arrest* and toured with him for just over three and a half years – at one point sharing the guitar duties with Mike Stern. After leaving the Davis band, Scofield built upon the exposure he had gained as a member of the trumpeter's group and released two further solo albums in the mid-1980s, *Electric Outlet* and *Still Warm*. Both albums helped reinforce his status in the jazz world.

In 1987, Scofield released the first of three albums featuring the powerful rhythm section of Dennis Chambers and Gary Grainger. The band, which had several different keyboard players, recorded the albums *Blue Matter*, *Loud Jazz* and *Pick Hits Live* and toured extensively. Scofield also found time to team up with fellow guitarist Bill Frisell in Marc Johnson's group Bass Desires to much critical acclaim.

In the early 1990s, Scofield formed a new quartet and signed with Blue Note Records to begin working with saxophonist Joe Lovano. He recorded *Time on My Hands* in 1990, with Lovano, bassist Charlie Haden and drummer Jack DeJohnette. The group replaced DeJohnette with Bill Stewart on drums and recorded another two albums before Scofield moved on to release the album *Grace Under Pressure*, once again teaming up with Bill Frisell. In 1994, Scofield continued his collaborations with other guitarists when he recorded *I Can See Your House From Here* with Pat Metheny.

By now predominantly playing music with a soul jazz or funk orientated sound, Scofield teamed up with organist Larry Goldings and bassist Dennis Irwin for his next group, releasing the albums *Hand Jive* and *Groove Elation*, both of which were critically well received. He also worked with the avant-garde trio Medeski, Martin and Wood in 1997 producing the *A Go Go* album.

Scofield began experimenting with modern drum 'n' bass rhythms by the early 2000s, releasing *Überjam* in 2002 and *Up All Night* in 2004. Also in 2004 he released *EnRoute: John Scofield Trio Live*, a trio recording with Steve Swallow on bass and Bill Stewart on drums. This was followed by a tribute album of music written by Ray Charles entitled *That's What I Say: John Scofield Plays the Music of Ray Charles*.

A second album with Medeski, Martin and Wood was released in 2006 and in 2010 he recorded the album *54*. Scofield's recording output continued with the album *A Moment's Peace* (released in 2011) once again featuring the playing of Larry Goldings alongside bassist Scott Colley and drummer Brian Blade.

Aside from his performing career and recording work, Scofield has also been involved in jazz education, most recently as a visiting professor within the jazz department at the Steinhardt School of Education in New York.

Scofield's playing style is instantly recognisable with a distinctive melodic vocabulary, often punctuated by his signature use of dissonant intervals and angular melodies. Like Pat Metheny, Scofield's soloing style is greatly admired by other musicians and he has emerged as one of the most individual sounding players of the modern era.

Scofield uses and endorses Ibanez guitars primarily and has a signature model, the JSM100. This guitar is designed around his long-time stage and recording guitar, a 1981 Ibanez AS200. He uses a variety of effects pedals including a Pro Co Rat distortion, along with various modulation and delay devices. For amplifiers he generally favours a Vox AC 30 or a Mesa Boogie combo and he also used Sundown amplifiers earlier in his career.

Recommended Listening

Rough House

Time on my Hands

A Go Go

John Scofield has an immediately identifiable style as a soloist, with a unique approach to note choice, phrasing and picking dynamics. This first example (played over the opening bars of the chord sequence known as the "Rhythm Changes") demonstrates how he can take a blues-based approach and give it a fresh and inventive makeover. Note the use of off-beat rhythms in the first two bars and also the small blues bends he frequently employs (see beats 2 and 3 in bar three).

Syncopated rhythms are a feature of bar four, mixing 1/4 notes, 1/8th notes and triplets before the lick concludes with a classic blues device: hammering onto the major 3rd of the Bb major chord. Make sure to refer to the audio to play the various rhythms accurately. Add some light overdrive to your guitar tone as well as a light chorus effect.

Example 18a

This next example stays with a blues based approach to Rhythm Changes, but with the addition of some chromatic passing notes (in bars one and two, on beats 3 and 2 respectively). As with the previous example, off-beat rhythms are a feature of the opening bar, before more syncopated rhythms appear in bar two, mixing 8th, 1/4 note and 1/16th note rhythms. In bar four is another of Scofield's favoured small blues bends, before the introduction of the dissonant sounding second interval on beat 2 of bar four.

Scofield frequently employs small interval phrases in his playing and is one of his signature soloing devices. The lick finishes with another major second interval on the up-beat of beat 2 in the final bar. Using a light overdrive with the bridge pickup selected (and perhaps with your tone control lowered a little) will give extra bite to these intervals.

Example 18b

You'll need to be somewhat careful with the rhythms in the first two bars of this next example and they may require some careful study along with the audio. Although the written pitch looks the same (bar one going into bar two) this motif uses the technique of playing the same sounding note on two different strings. Bar three is a typical blues phrase, culminating in a repeated hammer-on from 6th to the 7th fret on the G string (beat 2).

Bar four has a mixture of rhythms and you need to be especially careful of the timing of the final two triplets on beats 3 and 4, before finishing the line by holding over the last note into the first beat of the final bar.

Example 18c

This next example borrows several of the soloing approaches seen in the previous licks and again involves rhythmic syncopation and the use of small dissonant intervals. Watch out for the quick hammer-on figures on beat 4 of bar one and beat 1 of bar two. The trickiest phrase in this lick begins on the up-beat of beat 3 in bar two and continues until the tied note leading into the final bar. This line is easier to play than it looks on paper, so take your time and study the audio carefully to get the rhythms exactly right.

The lick concludes with the use of second intervals (bar four, beats 2, 3 and 4). Timing is crucial here, so if the written notation seems difficult to decipher, listen several times to the audio to hear how it should sound.

Example 18d

Scofield often uses specific intervals as a melodic motif in his playing, with sevenths being a particular favourite. This final lick begins with a 7th interval played from the 7th fret on the D string up to the 8th fret on the B string (which is bent up slightly). In bar two, a double-stop figure is bent slightly sharp to create a bluesy touch before the syncopated rhythms return on the up-beat of beat 2.

In bar three, watch out for the quarter note triplets over the final two beats and make sure you space them evenly. The final bar uses a common blues or RnB style blues lick, finishing on the b7 degree of the F7 chord.

Example 18e

19. Mike Stern

Mike Stern was born on January 10, 1953 in Boston, Massachusetts, and first became interested in learning guitar as a teenager growing up in Washington D.C. Stern's early musical influences were mostly rock and blues guitar players, but he later became increasingly attracted to the harmony and melodic language of jazz. His interest in studying jazz developed to the point where he subsequently returned to his native Boston to attend the prodigious Berklee College of Music. Whilst studying at Berklee, Stern's guitar playing skills soon attracted the attention of other like-minded jazz musicians and he became a regular performer on the local Boston jazz scene.

His first significant career break occurred when he was recommended (reputedly by Pat Metheny) to audition for the '70s rock group Blood Sweat and Tears and, after successfully passing the audition, he began touring with the band. Stern recorded two albums with BST and played with them for two years before eventually joining drummer Billy Cobham's high-energy fusion group Glass Menagerie in 1979. He remained with Cobham until early 1981 when he was recommended to the legendary trumpeter Miles Davis as the guitarist for Davis's new band. Stern played with Davis for three years in the early 1980s, recording two studio albums, *The Man with the Horn* and *Star People*, as well as the highly regarded live recording *We Want Miles*.

After leaving Davis's band, Stern played with former Weather Report bassist Jaco Pastorius in his Word of Mouth group and, after a brief period of rehabilitation to rid himself of drug and alcohol problems, he returned to play for another year with Miles Davis.

Stern recorded his first solo album *Neesh* in 1985 for the Japanese Trio label and a year later his first Atlantic Records jazz-fusion album *Upside Downside* was released to generally positive reviews from the music press. Stern's growing compositional skills, as well as his outstanding improvisational abilities, attracted a loyal fan base for him in the 1980s and his career maintained a steady climb upwards. After a brief period working with alto saxophonist David Sanborn in 1986, and some touring with the group Steps Ahead (featuring tenor saxophonist Michael Brecker), Stern joined forces with Brecker as part of the tenor player's own group, touring widely to great critical acclaim.

Stern continued to release jazz fusion-style solo albums during the late 1980s and early 1990s and he also formed a touring band with tenor saxophonist Bob Berg. In 1992 he was asked to play with the reformed Brecker Brothers group, once again alongside Michael Brecker. Stern also recorded an album of jazz standards in 1992 called *Standards and Other Songs* which showcased his bebop playing to great effect and was well-received by critics.

By the early 2000s, Stern had begun to explore the use of vocals on his solo recordings and after leaving Atlantic Records to sign with ESC Records, he continued his pattern of releasing solo recordings while still recording and playing with other jazz and fusion artists, including The Yellowjackets in 2008.

In 2014 Stern recorded and toured with Texas guitarist Eric Johnson in a highly successful collaboration. Stern suffered a major career setback in the summer of 2016 when he was badly injured in an accidental fall, but despite some serious injuries he has returned to live performance once more, although with a modified playing technique to help overcome his recent injuries. Stern has been nominated for and won multiple awards for his guitar playing and studio recordings and has released 17 solo albums to date.

Mike Stern played a both a Fender Stratocaster and a Telecaster early in his career, with the Telecaster model becoming his favoured guitar for many years. For much of the 1980s and 1990s he used a hybrid Telecaster built by Michael Aronson, based on an earlier instrument that was stolen from him. Stern has more recently been playing a Yamaha PA1511MS Mike Stern model guitar, based on the Aronson guitar. For amplification, Stern employs a stereo setup using an old Yamaha SPX90 and several Boss pedals played through twin amplifiers (usually Fender 65 Twin Reverbs).

Stern's playing style is a sophisticated amalgamation of bebop jazz vocabulary and often quite raw sounding blues/rock lines. This approach has been termed "Bop'n'Roll" by some critics and combines long bebop-style passages with traditional rock/blues bends and vibrato. Stern also uses improvisational devices and harmonic approaches more closely associated with horn players and jazz pianists than guitarists.

Recommended Listening

Play

Upside Downside

Standards (and other songs)

We Want Miles (Miles Davis)

Mike Stern uses a lot of blues phrases and pentatonic patterns in his soloing. This first lick employs the C Blues scale throughout. Beginning with a classic minor third motif on beat 1 of bar one, the quick 1/16th note triplet on beat 4 adds to the blues feel by featuring the b5 of the scale in a rapid hammer-on / pull off sequence. The lick concludes with a simple blues scale melody in bar three before finishing on the root of the Cm7 chord on the downbeat of bar four. Refer to the audio if the written rhythms look a little daunting and you'll soon hear how the example should sound.

Stern employs a stereo guitar sound with an SPX90 pitch shifter and two amplifiers for his main tone, but you can emulate his sound reasonably well for these examples by using a chorus effect.

Example 19a

Example 19b is a far cry from the simplicity of the previous example and demonstrates Stern's ability to superimpose multiple tonal centres over a single chord. Bar one features what jazz musicians refer to as "Coltrane changes" – a harmonic sequence popularised by saxophonist John Coltrane in the late 1950s. The angular sounding sequence is several triads/7th chord arpeggios moving from Eb Major on beat 1 through F#7, B7 to a four-note motif on D Major on beat 4.

This approach continues with a G Major arpeggio on beat 1 of bar two, before employing an Ebmaj7 arpeggio over the bar line between the second and third bars. Take your time learning this lick, as it may take a while for your ears to absorb some of the dissonance inherent in these kind of fusion jazz lines.

Example 19b

Like Pat Martino, Mike Stern often plays long 1/16th note passages in his solos and Example 19c is similar in style to Martino's approach. Two chromatic passing notes are employed on beats 1 and 3 of the first bar and the remaining notes are drawn from the C Aeolian mode – a Stern favourite for tonic minor chords.

Bar two begins with a 1/16th note triplet hammer-on / pull-off before continuing with the Aeolian scale. The lick finishes by targeting the minor 3rd and b7 degree of the Cm7 chord. Stern mostly uses alternate picking for this type of long melodic line, so practising your picking technique will certainly help to master this example.

Example 19c

Example 19d is almost exclusively based around arpeggios – another favourite improvisational device of Stern's. Beginning with a Bb triad alternating with an Ab triad in bar one, the line descends a long Ebmaj7 arpeggio. Watch that you play the correct rhythms in bar one, as they are slightly deceptive.

The line finishes with a short interval motif on the final beat of bar two before concluding on the root and b7 of the underlying Cm7 chord.

Example 19d

The final example is another lick that could have been played by Pat Martino and features 1/16th notes almost exclusively. There is a short scale sequence based on the C Melodic Minor scale on beats 1 and 2 of bar one, before some chromatic passing notes are added, taking the line up to the fast 1/16th note triplet at the beginning of bar two.

The line then uses the C Aeolian mode before landing on the 4th/11th of the Cm7 chord in bar three. Stern often mixes scale types in his solos to create different textures on the same chord, and this lick is a good example of how you can achieve this without it sounding awkward.

Example 19e

20. Pat Metheny

Patrick Bruce Metheny was born on August 12, 1954 in Lee's Summit, Missouri, into an already musical family. Metheny's father played trumpet (as did his brother) and his mother was a singer. After initially learning trumpet from his brother, Metheny grew increasingly attracted to the guitar. Inspired by a Beatles performance on TV, Metheny obtained his first guitar in 1964. He soon became especially drawn to the playing of Wes Montgomery and other jazz artists such as Miles Davis and before long he was performing regularly in his local area and practising continuously at home.

After winning a *Down Beat* magazine scholarship when he was only 15 years old, Metheny attended a summer camp with guitarist Attila Zoller and subsequently came to the attention of the Dean of the University of Miami, who offered him a scholarship at the University. Already regarded as something of a child prodigy, Metheny was soon teaching guitar, first in Florida and then at Berklee College of Music in Boston.

Metheny's recording debut was in 1974 on an album with pianist Paul Bley, bassist Jaco Pastorius, and drummer Bruce Ditmas, made for the Improvising Artists label. Metheny then joined vibraphonist Gary Burton's band in 1975, playing alongside fellow guitarist Mick Goodrick. In the following year, Metheny released his official debut album, *Bright Size Life* on the ECM label, again with Jaco Pastorius on bass. Metheny remained with the ECM for several years.

Metheny then formed the Pat Metheny Group, along with long-time collaborator, pianist Lyle Mays. The group released several albums over the next few years and their second recording, *American Garage*, successfully crossed over into the popular music charts, as well as reaching number one in the Billboard Jazz chart. A collaboration in the mid-1980s with David Bowie on *This is Not America* saw Metheny's music enter the top 40, both in the US and the UK.

The Metheny group evolved through several line-up changes in subsequent years and, after releasing the recording *First Circle*, Metheny left the ECM label and signed with the Geffen company for the album *Still Life (Talking)*. Despite solo and side projects, Metheny kept his main group together, although he moved away from more Latin influenced music to incorporate new and diverse instrumentation and compositional approaches.

Outside of the Pat Metheny Group, the guitarist has recorded numerous albums showcasing other sides of his musical personality, including *Secret Story* (his 1992 album using orchestral arrangements), *The Falcon and the Snowman* (a movie sound track from 1985), and the avant garde *Zero Tolerance for Silence* in 1994. He has also recorded with many other musicians including Dave Holland, Brad Mehldau, Michael Brecker, Joni Mitchell, Ornette Coleman, Jim Hall, Bruce Hornsby and bassist Marc Johnson to name just a few. He has also recorded on albums with his older brother, Mike Metheny, including *Day In – Night Out* (1986) and *Close Enough for Love* (2001).

In 2012, he formed the Unity Band with Antonio Sánchez on drums, Ben Williams on bass and Chris Potter on saxophone. This group toured Europe and the US and, in 2013, Metheny announced the formation of the Pat Metheny Unity Group, with the addition of the Italian multi-instrumentalist Giulio Carmassi.

Metheny has won countless awards for his music and his playing, including a staggering 20 Grammy Awards in ten separate categories.

A fluid and high inventive soloist with an instantly recognisable playing vocabulary, Metheny has emerged as one of the jazz greats of the modern era. With compositional skills as refined as his playing facility, he is one of the most revered (and imitated) modern jazz guitarists. His signature guitar sound is also much copied by contemporary players.

Metheny's choice of instrument depends much on the project he is involved with, although he generally favours his Ibanez PM signature model guitar. In the early part of his career he used a natural finish Gibson ES-175 before retiring the guitar in the mid-1990s. He has also used some highly unusual instruments designed especially for him, including a custom made 42-string Pikasso guitar. Metheny is also one of the most recognised users of the guitar synthesiser, particularly the Roland GR300. He regularly uses both six and twelve string acoustic guitars alongside his electric instruments.

Metheny used an Acoustic 134 amplifier for many years before switching to other brands including Digitech and Ashly. He also uses effects units such as the Lexicon Prime Time digital delay as an integral part of his signal chain.

Recommended Listening

Bright Size Life

Question and Answer (Pat Metheny/Dave Holland/Roy Haynes)

Still Life Talking (Pat Metheny Group)

Pat Metheny is a master of rhythmic phrasing across bar lines, so even though this lick looks simple on paper, it's important to keep your time steady throughout. The lick begins with a straightforward pentatonic pattern in C minor, which is moved up chromatically through the Dbmaj7 chord (in bars three and four) before resolving to C minor in bar five. Moving patterns like this is often referred to as "side-slipping" and is an effective way of momentarily playing outside of the key.

The dramatic single-note slides, such as beat 3 of bar six, are a signature feature of Metheny's playing and he will sometimes use double-stops, such as those on the first two beats of the final bar.

Example 20a

Metheny often employs repeating melodic patterns to great effect in his solos. Example 20b uses the same pattern from beat 3 of bar one, right through to bar three. Make sure to pull-off the middle two notes in each of these four-note phrases, as this helps to capture Metheny's legato approach.

Bar three features a bop-style melodic approach with a chromatic passing note on the up-beat of beat 3. This brings a contrast to earlier repeating pattern. The bop approach continues into bar four, before the line completes with a simple pentatonic motif in C minor.

Example 20b

Example 20c extends the "side-slipping" concept much further and uses one fingering pattern throughout. The pattern is moved up the fretboard chromatically on the same string set (G, B and E strings). In bar one, the pattern begins by targeting the 5th, b3, 9th and root of the C minor chord. It then ascends one fret at a time until the final two beats of the bar four. You will hear a good deal of dissonance in places with this lick, but this is intentional to create tension.

The final note of the lick (the high D note at the 10th fret) is there to release the previous harmonic tension (it is the 9th of the C minor chord). Using chromatic ascending patterns like this can be exciting in a solo, but they need to be used carefully. Always play them with a clear rhythm, otherwise it can just sound like you are playing wrong notes. Resolving to a chord tone after you have used some side-slipping is a wise move.

Example 20c

Although the next example is constructed from simple diatonic scales, it illustrates how Metheny produces a melodic solo by utilising clear rhythms and rock-solid phrasing. The first two bars only use notes from the C Minor Pentatonic scale, but the rhythmic placement of the notes makes all the difference. Instead of beginning on beat 1 of bar one, the line begins on beat 3 and includes a tied note across the bar line into bar two. In the third bar, just three notes are used to highlight the chord change to Dbmaj7. Notice the two beat rhythmic gap before the lick picks up again in bar four.

In bar five, the C Minor Pentatonic scale is employed once more with simple but effective alternating 1/4 and 1/8th note rhythms, before the lick completes with two 1/4 notes on bar seven. This kind of simple but strong phrasing really makes a line sound rhythmically interesting. Metheny employs this approach frequently in his solos, especially at faster tempos.

Example 20d

The final Pat Metheny example begins with two bars of silence before anything occurs. At medium-to-fast tempos, this can be a useful device. You can allow your solo time to develop, without playing constantly. The entrance at bar three over the Dbmaj7 chord is all the more dramatic after two bars of silence.

The line concludes with two typical Metheny finger-slides – first to the high Bb note on the B string (11th fret) and the C note on the same string at the 13th fret. There is nothing especially demanding here, but try to keep your time constant and don't be tempted to rush the phrases in this lick.

Example 20e

Sample Jazz Guitar Solo 1

This sample solo is played over a I VI II V chord progression in C major and incorporates four licks taken from the book. The I VI II V sequence is commonplace in jazz music and features in thousands of jazz standards. Building a solid vocabulary over this progression (preferably in all keys) is considered essential groundwork for any aspiring jazz musician.

The solo begins with the first lick from the Joe Pass chapter (Example 9a) and exhibits several classic bebop moves, such as the approach notes used to decorate the 5th and root of the Cmaj7 chord in bar one, through to the use of the b9 interval against the G7 chord in bar five. Almost every jazz musician would use altered tensions (b5, #5, b9 or #9) over the VI7 and V7 chords, as seen here. These altered tensions can be played singly or in combination with others.

The second lick effectively links to the first and is Example 6a from the Wes Montgomery chapter. This lick provides a welcome change in rhythmic structure from the opening four bars and the use of the 1/4 note triplets helps keep a relaxed "behind the beat" feel to the solo. Longer value triplet rhythms like this are often used by soloists to contrast with the more 1/8th and 1/16th note runs seen in many jazz solos.

Players such as Wes Montgomery frequently arranged their solos to feature chord work as well as single-note passages. The third featured lick in this sample solo uses such chord soloing, taken from Example 9c in the Joe Pass chapter. Using chord phrases like this can really help to add variety to a jazz solo and provide harmonic clarity. Be careful not to rush these chords when you play them – you might want to practise shifting from single notes to chords to get used to this approach. It will become second nature after a while and is a useful skill to develop on guitar.

Another Joe Pass lick ends this sample solo (Example 9e) and, in contrast to the first lick, uses 1/16th notes almost exclusively. This is sometimes referred to as double-time playing in jazz circles and can be dramatic if used musically. Pat Martino is an expert at playing long double-time 1/16th note lines, as of course was Joe Pass. Be aware of the fingering required to play the whole-tone based patterns in bar one and be careful not to rush the 1/16th notes in this long passage.

Example 21a

Sample Jazz Guitar Solo 2

Jazz solos aren't always played over multiple chord changes and many well-known jazz compositions feature solo sections comprising a single chord. This is sometimes referred to as a "one chord vamp". This second sample solo has only one chord (Cm9) to consider and therefore offers the soloist a lot of freedom in terms of their improvisational approach.

The solo begins with Example 19a (minus the pickup note) from the Mike Stern chapter and serves as a simple but melodically effective way to begin. The bluesy nature of this lick is accessible for an audience and many jazz solos over static chord vamps begin with blues-based phrases like this one. Remember to keep your time steady throughout and follow the hammer-on / pull-off directions on beat 4 of the first bar.

Lick two begins at bar five and is a Grant Green lick (Example 12b) combining 1/16th note triplets with off-beat 1/8th notes. Using repeated rhythmic and melodic motifs like this is a common approach on single chord vamps. The Ebmaj7 arpeggio used in bars six and seven is a chord substitution often applied to a Cm7 chord, so is particularly effective in this context.

The long 1/16th note line beginning at bar nine is again from the Mike Stern chapter (Example 19c). It is a great example of how you can use passing tones in an otherwise diatonic scale line to add chromatic tension to a solo. Stern is a master of this kind of embellished 1/16th note line played over a single chord. Watch for the small position shifts in this lick. Learn it by breaking it down into smaller sections at first.

The solo concludes with another Grant Green lick (Example 12a) and the emphasis here is on 1/8th note triplets. This lick is mostly played in 8th position, but watch out for the passage beginning on beat 3 of bar one5 – the triplets here are grouped in four rather than three. Refer to the audio to hear this rhythmic effect. Using different rhythmic groupings is another useful tool for the soloist, especially in single chord situations like this.

Example 21b

Conclusion

Well, there we have it! 100 awesome licks in the style of the world's greatest jazz guitar players. We hope you've enjoyed the journey and that you'll be dipping into this book for years to come.

As we mentioned in the introduction, you'll get the most from this book by making each lick your own. While it's valuable to copy the style of the musicians you love, you'll really benefit from shaping each lick to fit your own voice.

Experiment by changing the rhythm, phrasing, articulation and speed of any phrase to fit your musical personality. That's how language develops and it's how you'll create your own unique voice on the instrument. Just one lick can give you hours of creative pleasure in the practice room.

The best practice you can do is to perform these licks with a jam group, live or in a rehearsal room. The guitar feels different when you get away from the comfort of your backing tracks.

I'm proud to say that Fundamental Changes has now released over 100 guitar methods and some of those titles will help you develop and personalise your own language.

My book, **Blues Guitar Melodic Phrasing** takes a detailed look at how you can learn musical feel. I once asked a teacher how a famous guitarist played the way he did. He told me, "He's just feeling it." Well, maybe that was true, but it was a useless answer from a teacher! I set out to break down musical feel into a precise set of ideas and skills, and that study led to **Blues Guitar Melodic Phrasing**. Everything in there is completely applicable to jazz guitar too.

Some of the theoretical ideas in this book may be new to you. I try to keep the theory to a minimum and focus on the music. However, two books I've written to show the practical application of theory are **Guitar Scales in Context** and **The Practical Guide to Modern Theory for Guitarists**.

Both these books are extremely hands-on and really help with the day to day, musical application of theory.

If you're after some solid technical development, Simon Pratt's book **Guitar Finger Gym** is an awesome guide for most aspects of guitar technique, and my book **Complete Technique for Modern Guitar** is a good companion volume too.

Above all, have fun learning the music that you love. If you're not smiling, you're doing it wrong!

Joseph

Learn Jazz with Martin Taylor

Master Jazz Guitar Chord Melody with Virtuoso Martin Taylor MBE

Beyond Chord Melody with Martin Taylor MBE condenses over 40 years of playing expertise and insight into this beautiful jazz guitar book. Learn from the internationally acclaimed master of jazz chord melody guitar as he guides you through his 7-step method to creating your own guitar arrangements.

As a special bonus, 2 specially commissioned online videos are included, with Martin illustrating key techniques.

What you'll learn:

- 7 steps to jazz chord melody guitar that will unlock your creativity

- How to make a chord melody arrangement of any jazz standard.

- How to play chords and solo at the same time.

- Overcome the common blocks that stifle your progress

- Build stunning jazz chord melody guitar arrangements

- The essential components of any jazz standard

- Break away from chord boxes and discover the freedom of polyphonic guitar playing

Beyond Chord Melody teaches you Martin Taylor's own secret formula for creating instant jazz guitar arrangements and gives you the tools to master your guitar and create your own stunning chord melody arrangements.

This book is the antidote to formulaic guitar methods. His 7-step chord melody guitar system helps you "break out of the box" and is taught in a clear, concise manner.

About Pete Sklaroff

Pete Sklaroff is a freelance guitarist, author, teacher and studio musician with over 30 years professional experience in the music industry. He is also the former Assistant Head of Music and Head of Jazz Studies at Leeds College of Music in the UK.

Pete operates a highly successful online guitar teaching practice and has taught hundreds of guitarists over the years. He is a long-time collaborator with Fundamental Changes, recording many of the audio examples for their successful guitar publications and is a much sought after studio musician.

Pete can be contacted via his website: **www.petesklaroff.com**

Other Jazz Books from Fundamental Changes

For further study of jazz and to get more ideas about how to apply these licks, check out the following books from Fundamental Changes.

- **Beyond Chord Melody with Martin Taylor**

- **Chord Tone Soloing for Jazz Guitar**

- **Fundamental Changes in Jazz Guitar**

- **Minor ii V Mastery**

- **Voice Leading Jazz Guitar**

- **Bebop Jazz Blues Guitar**

- **Jazz Blues Soloing for Guitar**

www.ingramcontent.com/pod-product-compliance
Lightning Source LLC
Chambersburg PA
CBHW081431090426
42740CB00017B/3261